THE PASSIONATE OBSERVER

Self-Portrait, March 9, 1934

THE PASSIONATE OBSERVER

Photographs by Carl Van Vechten

KEITH F. DAVIS

Hallmark Cards, Inc.

Kansas City, Missouri

This publication is one of a series from the Hallmark Photographic Collection celebrating the history and art of photography. Previous titles include *Todd Webb: Photographs of New York and Paris, 1945-1960* (1986), *Harry Callahan: New Color, Photographs 1978-1987* (1988), *George N. Barnard: Photographer of Sherman's Campaign* (1990), and *Clarence John Laughlin: Visionary Photographer* (1990).

The Hallmark Photographic Collection is a selected survey of the history of modern photography. Begun in 1964, it now includes over 2300 original prints by 300 of this century's most significant photographers. The collection reflects Hallmark's long tradition of support for the visual arts and its interest in making positive and original contributions to contemporary cultural life. The sharing of this resource through domestic and international traveling exhibitions is a fundamental part of this larger company philosophy. Since 1980 forty exhibitions have been presented in over 200 bookings in leading museums across the United States, and in Canada, Australia, New Zealand, Great Britain, and Switzerland.

With the exception of figures 2 and 3 all images reproduced in this book are from original prints in the Hallmark Photographic Collection. Figures 2 and 3 are from the Carl Van Vechten Papers, Rare Books and Manuscripts Division, New York Public Library, Astor, Lenox and Tilden Foundations.

The photographs of Carl Van Vechten are reproduced with the kind permission of Mr. Joseph Solomon, executor of the artist's estate.

The work by George Platt Lynes, illustrated as figure 9, is reproduced courtesy the Estate of George Platt Lynes.

This book was designed by Malcolm Grear Designers, Providence, Rhode Island, with separations by Richard Benson and Thomas Palmer, Newport, Rhode Island, and printing by Meridian Printing of East Greenwich, Rhode Island.

Distributed by the University of New Mexico Press, Albuquerque, New Mexico

ISBN: 0-87529-668-8 (cloth)
          0-87529-669-6 (paper)

Printed in the United States of America

CONTENTS

INTRODUCTION
AND
ACKNOWLEDGMENTS

Carl Van Vechten was a man of many talents and enormous vitality. In a professional life that spanned the first seven decades of the twentieth century he led no fewer than three creative "lives"–as critic, novelist, and photographer. With characteristic verve, Van Vechten threw himself completely into each of these successive endeavors. His boundless energy, unorthodox tastes, and flamboyant sense of style resulted in a remarkably large body of original and insightful work.

Van Vechten played a uniquely complex role in the artistic culture of his era. He was considerably more prominent in his day than his current reputation would suggest. He was, in fact, a prototypically modern sort of celebrity, famous both for his artistic ability and his social visibility. Van Vechten was a respected creative talent as well as an indefatigable participant in the giddy social life of, in his phrase, "the splendid drunken twenties." He celebrated the cultural importance of the artistic process and the personal vitality of creative individuals. Fascinated by the chemistry of interpersonal contact, he cultivated friendships with many of the most noted figures of his day.

In addition to his roles as artist and *bon vivant*, however, Van Vechten considered himself a reasonably objective witness to his era–an historian of its manners and spirit. This double role as both participant and observer gives his work an unexpected dimension. He celebrated the high life and good times while remaining gently skeptical of them. Respected as a creative artist in his own right, Van Vechten devoted remarkable energy to promoting the talents of others. And, while attuned to the most subtle nuances of style, he was able to view himself and his culture in a much larger historical frame of reference. It is this curious dual perspective, in large measure, that makes Van Vechten's legacy so intriguing.

Van Vechten's sense of history was expressed, in part, in his amassing of documents of all kinds. His penchant for collecting and preserving began in childhood and remained central to his life's work. As a youth he collected birds' nests, postage stamps, and tobacco tags. In adulthood, his accumulative activities focused on his professional interests of music and literature. Van Vechten's steadily growing archive of publications, correspondence, and ephemera provided data for his writing, which, in turn, grew into a unique chronicle of his era. Van Vechten's critical essays of the 1910s comprise a valuable record of some of the most creative personalities of the day. His novels of the 1920s similarly provide an insightful perspective on the mood and manners of a particularly vibrant cultural era.

Beginning in the late 1930s, Van Vechten created several important public collections from the material he had accumulated in the preceding decades. These archives include the James Weldon Johnson Memorial Collection of Negro Arts and Letters at Yale University, the George Gershwin Memorial Collection of Music and Musical Literature and the Florine Stettheimer Memorial Collection of Books about the Fine Arts, both at Fisk University, and collections of his own letters, literary material, and photographs at Yale, the New York Public Library, the Museum of the City of New York, the Museum of Modern Art, and the University of New

Mexico. Van Vechten's generous support of these and other collections continued in his later life.

Van Vechten's work with the camera forms a central, if often underrated, aspect of his enormous oeuvre. Between 1932 and his death in 1964 he made more than 15,000 photographs. In these years Van Vechten turned the great bulk of his expressive energy to photography, using the medium to synthesize perfectly his most basic creative concerns. The camera brought to particularly eloquent focus his fascination for celebrities, penchant for collecting, and enthusiasm for personal and artistic style.

In addition to their many individual pleasures, Van Vechten's photographs form an invaluable chronicle of the arts and letters of his time. In its entirety, Van Vechten's work with the camera provides monumental testimony to the diversity of human creativity. His artistic vision was founded on a belief in the primacy of the talented individual and a recognition of the varied backgrounds, temperaments, and tastes from which such accomplishment could arise.

Van Vechten's photographic work also reflects his deep faith in the importance of cultural memory. He commemorated the noted personalities of his era in order to preserve for future generations something of their spirit and physical presence. By depicting some of the most gifted figures of his time, Van Vechten's photographs encourage us to value a spectrum of past accomplishment. They may also remind us of the varied human resources of our own era.

Despite the activities of several devoted champions, Van Vechten's photographic work remains underappreciated today. Several causes for this relative neglect may be suggested. During his entire career as a photographer Van Vechten worked as an amateur with no need to promote or profit from his work. While his pictures were exhibited, published, and praised in their day, the basic nature of Van Vechten's activity remained considerably more private than public. It is also significant that Van Vechten died in 1964, roughly a decade before the advent of any significant art market for individual photographic prints. In the years before and after his death large groups of photographs were donated to various institutions. Ironically, the very definitiveness of some of these collections has probably hampered an artistic appraisal of his work. It is a daunting task, for example, to survey the more than 12,000 prints given to the Philadelphia Museum of Art by Van Vechten's friend Mark Lutz.

It is also true that Van Vechten's prolificacy resulted in images of widely varying quality. He typically made many exposures in the course of his photographic sessions and printed a surprisingly large percentage of the resulting negatives. A considerable number of favorite subjects were recorded numerous times over many years. While the resulting body of work is of great value to the historian, it tends to frustrate the connoisseur's desire to identify, for example, Van Vechten's "definitive" portrait of George Gershwin from the dozen or more he made, or the best of his hundreds of images of the dancer Alicia Markova. And since Van Vechten was more interested in his subjects than in the making of precious and meticulous prints, the resulting images differ in both technical quality and aesthetic appeal.

At its best, however, Van Vechten's work brings together a lively personal vision, eloquently expressive prints, and a tangible sympathy for his sitters. For all their technical simplicity, Van Vechten's photographs beautifully convey the presence of his subjects—whether the exotic elegance of actress Anna May Wong, the exuberant vitality of musician Cab Calloway, or the practiced theatricality of stage star Judith Anderson. These pictures reveal Van Vechten's considerable powers of observation and his interest in the personalities he recorded. A great many of his photographs are doubly thoughtful, suggesting both the analytical nature of Van Vechten's vision and the reflective depth of his subjects. He genuinely admired the people he photographed, and this feeling, in combination with his visual intelligence and sense of style, resulted in a body of work of both historic and artistic importance.

The present volume provides a fresh overview of this fascinating body of work. The photographs reproduced on the following pages were carefully chosen for the Hallmark Photographic Collection from a much larger group. This selection was made for the clarity of its thematic focus—on portraiture, the most important aspect of Van Vechten's photographic work—and the breadth of its thirty-year chronological span. While far from exhaustive, it is hoped that this selection succeeds in providing a persuasive argument for the significance of Carl Van Vechten's photographic career.

This book, and the accompanying exhibition, could not have been accomplished without the assistance of many knowledgeable and generous people. Deep thanks go to George Rinhart for bringing this body of work to my attention, eloquently outlining its importance, and sharing related documentary material. I am enormously grateful to Bruce Kellner, the leading scholar of Van Vechten's career, for his enthusiasm for this project, his tireless help on innumerable matters of fact and interpretation, and his willingness to read preliminary drafts of the following essay. Professor Kellner's crystalline memory and fine publications on Van Vechten were invaluable to this study. Great appreciation is also extended to Donald Gallup, Literary Trustee to the Estate of Carl Van Vechten, and retired Curator of the Collection of American Literature in the Yale University Library, for his encouragement and cooperation. Similar thanks are due the executor of Van Vechten's estate, Joseph Solomon, of the firm Gallet, Dreyer & Berkey, for permission to reproduce the photographs in this volume. My research in the Van Vechten collections of Yale University Library, the New York Public Library, and the Philadelphia Museum of Art were greatly facilitated, respectively, by Steve Jones, Valerie Wingfield, and Martha Chahroudi, and sincere thanks are extended to all. Gratitude is also due Deborah Willis, for help in the early stages of this project, and to Annasue McCleave Wilson for editorial advice.

The production of this volume represents a happy collaboration of some exceptionally talented people. The book was designed with characteristic sensitivity by Malcolm Grear Designers, Providence, Rhode Island, and carefully printed by the staff of Meridian Printing, East Greenwich, Rhode Island. The separations were skillfully produced by Richard Benson and Thomas Palmer, of Newport, Rhode Island. Deep thanks are extended to all.

Sincere gratitude is also due Hallmarkers Pat Fundom, Melissa Rountree, Mike Pastor, Jaye Wholey, and Rich Vaughn for their help with various aspects of this production. I am also deeply appreciative of the consistent support and guidance of William A. Hall, Assistant to the Chairman.

This is the eighth major publication from the Hallmark Photographic Collection, and the touring exhibition it accompanies is about the fortieth to be assembled from our corporate fine art holdings over the last dozen years. In its longevity, quality, and commitment to a broad public audience, this program has few peers in the corporate world. The commitment to scholarship and the arts upon which this activity rests is a direct expression of the values of the directing officers of Hallmark Cards, Inc.: Irvine O. Hockaday, President and Chief Executive Officer, and Donald J. Hall, Chairman of the Board.

KEITH F. DAVIS
Fine Art Programs Director
Hallmark Cards, Inc.

A PRIVILEGED EYE

The Life and Photographs of Carl Van Vechten

Carl Van Vechten began life in Cedar Rapids, Iowa. He was born in 1880, the third and last child of Charles and Ada Van Vechten. He was far younger than his brother and sister–eighteen and sixteen years, respectively–and so received the attention of an only child. Shortly after his birth, the economic fortunes of the Van Vechten family improved dramatically and Carl was raised in considerable comfort in an imposing three-story Victorian house. His father, a graduate of Columbia Law School, was a successful insurance broker and banker. Van Vechten's mother was an early proponent of women's rights and an advocate of the arts.

The Van Vechten household was one of the most cultured in Cedar Rapids. The young Carl grew up surrounded by literature, music, and an awareness of larger social issues. He loved books and became a regular patron of the Cedar Rapids Public Library, which had been founded by his mother. He read Shakespeare, Dickens, Horatio Alger, Jr., Henry James, George Bernard Shaw, Mark Twain, Ibsen, *The Arabian Nights*, *Swiss Family Robinson*, and a variety of popular dime novels. He also displayed an early interest in music, learning to play Schubert, Beethoven, and Bizet on the family's rosewood grand piano. In high school Van Vechten's interests turned to theater, and he wrote and performed in several plays.

His passion for the stage was stimulated by the productions he attended at the opera house in his home town. Cedar Rapids was midway between Chicago and Omaha and nearly every touring theater company stopped to perform there. These productions–primarily musicals and light operas–formed some of the happiest memories of Van Vechten's youth. Fascinated by the glamour and talent of these performers, he began an extensive collection of cigarette pictures and autographs of actresses. While this passion for cataloging stemmed naturally from his earlier interests in accumulating birds' nests, stamps, and tobacco tags, it marked the beginning of an abiding fascination for artistic celebrities.

These interests only emphasized Van Vechten's difference from his peers. He was an ungainly adolescent: six feet tall at the age of thirteen, with protruding front teeth that defied straightening. From the time of his youth Van Vechten began cultivating and flaunting his uniqueness. He became known in Cedar Rapids for his urbane sense of fashion. He wore a derby and narrow patent-leather boots, and "had the highest collars and tightest trousers in town."[1] Van Vechten's flamboyant sense of style became a lifelong trademark. In his maturity he was never seen without gold and jade bracelets, brilliantly colored shirts, and outrageous ties.[2]

The 1890s was the age of the dandy, and Van Vechten exemplified this brand of upper-class bohemianism. The American dandy represented a synthesis of two dissimilar concepts: the Victorian notion of the self-made man–the Horatio Alger archetype who achieved success through sheer will and imagination–and the mystical, anti-modernist rejection of the practical world espoused by the European decadents and Symbolists. The turn-of-the-century dandy was a spiritual aristocrat, a self-made artistic being who stood elegantly on the margins of mainstream society. Detached and observant, the dandy disdained mundane reality for a life of aesthetic refinement.

The roots of these ideas were elegantly expressed in Charles Baudelaire's important essay, "The Painter of Modern Life," first published in 1863. Baudelaire celebrated the inherent modernity of the dandy's attitude and his sensitivity to the moral and aesthetic flavor of his time. Baudelaire's dandy was a man of unending curiosity and deep enthusiasm for the "grace" of contemporary life. A creature of the modern city, he found in the congested vitality of the crowd "an immense reservoir of electrical energy," and sought a continual sense of "intoxication" from life and art.[3] Baudelaire's dandy took endless pleasure in "the outward show of life"–the pageantry of aristocratic existence and military processions, the conventions of the theater and women's fashion, the rituals of courtship and love, and the amusements of urban night life. These emblems of modernity were both mysterious and enchanting to Baudelaire's "passionate observer."

This attitude implied a profound sense of privilege. Baudelaire stated that the dandy's only occupation was "the perpetual pursuit of happiness....These beings have no other calling but to cultivate the idea of beauty in their persons, to satisfy their passions, to feel and to think."[4] These ideas both reflected and encouraged a cult of the self. Baudelaire wrote of "the burning need to create for oneself a personal originality." The dandy's ultimate goal was the choreographed presentation of "an artistically composed self."[5]

There was a fascinating duality in this carefully constructed pose. Even at its most flamboyant and carefree, the dandy's stance represented "a conspiracy of observed and observer in the same skin."[6] As Baudelaire noted, dandyism "is the joy of astonishing others, and the personal satisfaction of never oneself being astonished," as proof of having already seen and done it all.[7] The dandy's self-conscious synthesis of presentation and observation blurred the distinction between theater and the world. Life became another kind of role-playing with its own artificialities, conventions, and transformative possibilities.

By the turn of the century the look and affectations of the dandy had become broadly fashionable among the young, poetic, and comfortably disenchanted. However, at its most genuine, as in Van Vechten's case, this stance continued to have meaning by symbolizing a dedication to sensual pleasure, intellectual curiosity, ironic detachment, aesthetic refinement, and the celebration of the self as an artistic construct.[8]

After graduating from high school in 1899, Van Vechten eagerly left Cedar Rapids for the University of Chicago and the attractions of the big city. He majored in English but spent at least as much time on social and cultural amusements as he did on his studies. He regularly visited the city's art galleries, theaters, and ragtime bars, and savored performances by the Chicago Symphony Orchestra and several visiting opera companies.[9] Musical and literary pursuits dominated his interests. Before graduating in 1903 he composed several musical scores and contributed essays to the *University of Chicago Weekly*.

Van Vechten's growing interest in writing led to his first profession as a journalist. After receiving his university degree, Van Vechten accepted a job with the *Chicago American* newspaper. As a cub reporter he covered a wide range of subjects: from disastrous fires and a Presidential campaign to gossip on society and theater personalities. He moved to New York in 1906 and was commissioned by Theodore Dreiser, the editor of *Broadway Magazine*, to write on Richard

Strauss's controversial opera *Salome*. He was then hired as a reporter by the *New York Times* and, in addition to his routine duties, began taking assignments declined by the *Times*'s conservative music critic, Richard Aldrich. In the course of this work Van Vechten came to know the leading opera and musical personalities of the day.

Van Vechten's ability as a writer and his knowledge of the dramatic arts increased steadily in the following years. In 1908-09 he served as the *Times*'s correspondent in Paris, and was invigorated by that city's cultural life. In addition to writing on theater and opera, he interviewed Rodin, saw the Wright brothers fly, and reported (with less enthusiasm) on such routine subjects as sports, politics, crime, and fashion. Upon resuming his former duties in New York, Van Vechten continued to write on opera and theater for the *Times* while contributing to publications such as *New Music Review*. Performances by Isadora Duncan in late 1909 and Anna Pavlova in early 1910 stimulated his interest in modern dance and ballet, and Van Vechten's ecstatic praise of these artists earned him the title of America's first dance critic.[10]

Van Vechten's natural gregariousness, in combination with his duties for the *Times*, resulted in a steadily expanding circle of acquaintances in New York and overseas. In February 1913 he met Mabel Dodge, a wealthy patron of the arts, and the two immediately became friends. Van Vechten was stimulated by Dodge's taste and original sense of style, while she enjoyed his passionate enthusiasm for the new, unusual, and daring. Van Vechten accompanied Dodge on visits to the famed Armory Show of controversial modern art, and became a regular at the "evenings" in her apartment at 23 Fifth Avenue.

Dodge's gatherings were a lively potpourri of "socialists and suffragettes, artists and atheists, poets and journalists, and free thinkers and free lovers" engaged in animated discussion of a variety of artistic and cultural issues.[11] Here Van Vechten came to know and share opinions with many of the leading writers, thinkers, and artists of the day. These included personalities as diverse as photographer and arts empressario Alfred Stieglitz, the painters Marsden Hartley and Francis Picabia, the writer Lincoln Steffens and journalist Hutchins Hapgood, playwright Avery Hopwood, music critic Pitts Sanborn, birth control advocate Margaret Sanger, and political activists John Reed and Emma Goldman. These evenings were, in effect, a "combination of town meeting, bohemian Chatauqua, and cocktail party," and all in attendance were stimulated by the diversity of Dodge's guest list.[12]

While Van Vechten met some of these people for the first time at Dodge's house, he contributed significantly to the vitality of her evenings. His duties with the *Times*, and particularly his "Monday interviews" with personalities of the day, gave him "entrée to the most glittering scenes in the world of dance, music, and theater."[13] By introducing a variety of critics, playwrights, actors, singers, and poets to Dodge's evenings he greatly enlivened the creative community's social and intellectual exchanges.

One of Van Vechten's most enduring friendships was the result of an introduction from Mabel Dodge. In Paris, in the early summer of 1913, he met Gertrude Stein, an American expatriate esteemed by the literary avant-garde for the odd genius and hermetic difficulty of her writing. An immediate and lifelong fellowship was begun (figure 1; plate 26). On this visit Van Vechten saw several of Sergei Diaghilev's ballets, featuring the astounding dancing of Nijinsky, and attended Igor Stravinsky's landmark *Le*

1   Unidentified Photographer: *Carl Van Vechten and Gertrude Stein at the Poe Shrine in Richmond*, February 7, 1935

Sacre du Printemps. These experiences were profoundly moving, and reinforced Van Vechten's faith in the importance and transformative power of avant-garde art.

Following a season's stint as drama editor for the *New York Press*, from September 1913 to May 1914, Van Vechten returned to Europe amid the threat of impending war. His companion on this trip was Fania Marinoff, a dark-haired American actress of Russian birth (figure 4; plate 24). The two were married a few months later and began an elegantly impoverished life together in New York. The young couple survived, marginally, on Marinoff's acting jobs and Van Vechten's intermittent editing and writing assignments. Their lives were complicated by a suit brought by Van Vechten's former wife (a failed marriage that had lasted from 1907 to 1912). Unable to pay alimony, he spent a good-spirited and relatively comfortable month in the city's Ludlow Street jail. While incarcerated, Van Vechten wrote essays for such publications as Marcel Duchamp's odd magazine *Blindman*, and contributed to the *New York Evening Sun*.

Van Vechten was released from jail in April of 1915, in debt and unemployed. The nation was preoccupied by the increasingly bloody war in Europe, and the outlets for freelance criticism were few and unprofitable. While he continued to publish in periodicals such as *Seven Arts*, *Vanity Fair*, and *Smart Set*, Van Vechten decided to rework and compile the best of his essays into book form. This interest expanded into a five-year project. Between 1915 and 1920, Van Vechten published seven volumes of new and collected critical essays: *Music After the Great War and Other Studies* (1915), *Music and Bad Manners* (1916), *Interpreters and Interpretations* (1917), *The Merry-Go-Round* (1918), *The Music of Spain* (1918), *In the Garrett* (1919), and a slightly revised version of the first half of his 1917 volume, *Interpreters* (1920). These were followed several years later by two volumes of selections from his earlier books: *Red: Papers on Musical Subjects* (1925) and *Excavations: A Book of Advocacies* (1926).

These books chart their author's evolving tastes and interests. The earliest were exclusively devoted to musical subjects, while the later ones embraced a variety of artistic topics. Included in these volumes are essays celebrating black theater, spirituals, and jazz, contemporary artists

such as Igor Stravinsky, Nijinsky, and Erik Satie, and the possibilities for modern music in the new medium of film. Van Vechten's mature style is suggested clearly in these pieces: his penchant for lists, quotations, obscure sources, whimsy, and enthusiastic discoveries. He argued the larger importance of such popular composers as Irving Berlin, and for reappraisals of the obscure novelist Henry Blake Fuller and of the underappreciated later work of Herman Melville.

Despite their unevenness in quality and originality, these pieces strongly evoke the breadth of Van Vechten's reading, his passion for uncommon personalities and experiences, and his underlying persuasive intent. He took an emotional rather than academic approach to his subjects, and wrote in an "urbane and impressionistic" style.[14] Van Vechten assumed the "hybrid role of critic, gossip columnist, and press agent," and as a result his writing is more notable for its enthusiasm than for its analytical depth.[15] However, by conveying his own passion for certain artists or works, Van Vechten hoped to encourage his readers to make similar discoveries on their own. What mattered to him was the very personal and vibrant experience of art, and not its intellectual dissection.

While they typically received thoughtful and positive reviews, none of these books were best sellers, and Van Vechten's finances remained uncertain. For this reason, and because he felt he had already expressed the gist of his critical vision, Van Vechten embarked on new writing projects in 1919. The first of these was a lengthy book on cats, a subject of great personal interest. His collected lore on the history of the feline and its relation to the various arts was published as *The Tiger in the House* (1920). An immediate critical and popular success, *Tiger* has been reissued over the years in several editions.

Van Vechten then turned to the writing of fiction, an idea he had been contemplating for several years. His professional career as a novelist occupied the entire decade of the 1920s. Between 1922 and 1930 he published seven works of fiction: *Peter Whiffle* (1922), *The Blind Bow-Boy* (1923), *The Tattooed Countess* (1924), *Firecrackers* (1925), *Nigger Heaven* (1926), *Spider Boy* (1928), and *Parties* (1930). These books were, on the whole, both critical and popular successes. The first of these, *Peter Whiffle*, went through fifteen printings by the end of the decade and proved moderately profitable. The success of subsequent volumes increased his economic security and sense of artistic freedom.

While these books deal with a variety of subjects, they are clearly linked by Van Vechten's style and basic ideas. The works are almost uniformly light, stylish, and witty, with delicate counterpoints of cynicism and irony. They typically combine quickly paced narration with a familiar set of literary devices. In jacket copy written for *Firecrackers*, Van Vechten slyly lampooned both his style and criticism of it:

> Another of Carl Van Vechten's unimportant, light novels, disfigured by all of this author's customary annoying mannerisms: choice of a meaningless title, rejection of quotation marks, adoption of obsolete or unfamiliar words, an obstinate penchant for cataloguing, and an apparent refusal to assume a reverent attitude towards the ideals of life which are generally held most precious.

Most of his novels were strongly autobiographical, evoking Van Vechten's personal "enthusiasms for art, beauty, youth, rich eccentrics, great ladies, exquisite settings, clothes, and the 'forbidden.'"[16] He wrote of what he knew through experience: the New York of his day, the discovery of Paris as a young man, and the claustrophobia of small midwest cities. People he knew in actual life populate his novels under their own names or transparent pseudonyms. In his first novel Mabel Dodge becomes "Edith Dale," while Theodore Dreiser, Alfred Stieglitz, and a host of other noted acquaintances make fleeting appearances. Van Vechten's tastes in painting, music, and literature are echoed by his characters, and his love of parties, nightlife, and colorful personalities is everywhere apparent.

The self-referential nature of these books is underscored by Van Vechten's frequent use of himself as a character. He is the first-person narrator of *Peter Whiffle*, a thinly disguised Paul Moody ("a young man of good character but no moral sense...who went to Ludlow [Street jail] for refusing to pay his wife alimony") in *The Blind Bow-Boy*, and the midwestern writer Gareth Brooks in three other novels.[17] In other instances he wrote of himself in the third person as a recognized public figure. His name appears at the end of *Spider Boy*, for example, in a list of New York celebrities that a star-struck character in the novel longs to meet.

The self-reflexivity of Van Vechten's fiction is both narcissistic and genuinely clever. The story line of his featherweight farce on Hollywood, *Spider Boy: A scenario for a moving picture*, curls back on itself to form a kind of narrative Möbius strip. The tension between truth and illusion lies at the heart of the tale, as description and invention blur hopelessly together. Appearances are never what they seem: close examination reveals that the impressive "stone" facades of Hollywood buildings are stucco, while the elegant guests attending the central character's wedding party are recognized as studio extras. Van Vechten's story centers on a writer who cannot write and the creation of a screenplay that is spectacularly unusable. By the end of the book, however, the absurdity of the writer's failure becomes, in itself, an ironic simulacrum of any number of actual films of the period. Indeed, the book's odd slapstick episodes and impossibly happy ending only make sense as parodies of the simplistic formulas of Hollywood movies. By provoking complex thoughts on various kinds of representation, this "light" novel amply demonstrates Van Vechten's stated desire to treat "extremely serious themes as frivolously as possible."[18]

Van Vechten's urbane and sophisticated style had a distinctive mood. While deeply irreverent and sardonic, he never ventured into the darkly pessimistic terrain explored by other, more disillusioned, writers of his time.

> [Van Vechten] was a sociable observer and participant and not a neurasthenic who pursued...the personal themes of loss and isolation which preoccupied so many artists of the era. The tragic conflict of the sensitive individual in twentieth-century society was nearly always the basis of his work, but he refused to have his books weighted down with a sense of despair or *angst*.[19]

This approach stemmed in part from the fact that Van Vechten had not been traumatized by service in the world war. Most importantly, however, it reflected the coolly bemused stance of the true dandy. Van Vechten's attitude is succinctly expressed by a character in *The Blind Bow-Boy* who ruminates that

> the tragedies of life...were either ridiculous or sordid. The only way to get the sense of this absurd, contradictory, and perverse existence into a book was to withdraw entirely from reality. The artist who feels the most poignantly the bitterness of life wears a persistent and sardonic smile.[20]

Van Vechten celebrated the worldly pleasures of life while, at the same time, calmly viewing the foibles of contemporary existence from a psychological arm's length. His books celebrate the enlightened pleasures of an upper-class bohemianism while suggesting the frivolous and unreflective qualities of that life. Comfortable with himself and his existence, Van Vechten took little interest in popular causes, and resisted all rigid points of view. His books evoke a variety of powerful ideas, but these concepts are generally expressed subtly, within the fabric of simple narratives.

For all these virtues, however, the current obscurity of Van Vechten's novels suggests the limitations of his talent. His stylistic mannerisms and topical references have not remained uniformly interesting, and it is too easy to interpret his deliberate lightness of effect as simply superficial. Few of his books can be said truly to "transcend" the circumstances of their creation and original appreciation. However, a great deal of the value of this work lies precisely in the fact that it is so fully *of* its time. Van Vechten's most significant books combined an elite and often esoteric sensibility with "best-seller" popularity. They are a peculiarly evocative record of the ideas and tastes of an increasingly distant age and deserve, if for no other reason than this, to be remembered.[21]

Van Vechten's most serious and controversial novel, *Nigger Heaven*, appeared in August 1926. The book was a bestseller and the subject of widely mixed critical opinions. White audiences, on the whole, praised its mixture of sensationalism and realism. A number of influential black intellectuals also applauded the honesty of Van Vechten's portrayal of both the best and worst of Harlem life. Its publication marked the first time a noted white writer had taken black Harlem as a subject and this, too, seemed cause for celebration. However, many other Harlem residents condemned the novel with varying degrees of passion. Most took understandable offense at the book's title without reading beyond the cover or acknowledging Van Vechten's genuine empathy for his subject.[22] These critics condemned his depiction of black life as the lurid vision of a commercially-motivated literary voyeur. In truth, *Nigger Heaven* was a mixed success. Although clearly not Van Vechten's best book, it did contain more complexity and insight than its critics acknowledged.[23]

The mixed reception of the book could not obscure the fact that Van Vechten's interest in black American culture was genuine and deeply rooted. While his contacts with African-Americans were limited in Cedar Rapids, he had been raised to abhor racial prejudice. His interest in African-American music–spirituals, ragtime, and jazz–was well-established by 1919, when he wrote an essay on "The Negro Theater." By about 1924 he had discovered the cultural pleasures of Harlem and spent a great deal of time carousing in its speakeasies, clubs, and theaters. He also developed warm friendships with such noted African-Americans as NAACP official and black activist James Weldon Johnson, the singer and actor Paul Robeson, and poet Langston Hughes.

Van Vechten became a familiar figure in Harlem and its most visible white booster. He wrote several articles on black singers and music for publications such as *Vanity Fair*. He also personally encouraged and promoted a number of talented African-American writers, actors, and musicians. Through his efforts, for example, Alfred A. Knopf published Langston Hughes's first volume, *The Weary Blues*, as well as books by Nella Larsen and Rudolph Fisher. Van Vechten also made major contributions to racial understanding through his endless social activities. He introduced many of his peers to the culture of black New York, and became known as "white America's guide to Harlem."[24]

Just as significantly, Van Vechten brought a steady stream of black friends and acquaintances south of 110th Street to social gatherings at his west side apartment. While not unprecedented, his integrated "evenings" were very unusual for their time and nearly always memorable. On any given night George Gershwin, Bessie Smith, Ethel Waters, or Paul Robeson might perform for an audience that included Somerset Maugham, Tallulah Bankhead, Theodore Dreiser, F. Scott Fitzgerald, Adele Astaire, and Miguel Covarrubias. Van Vechten's parties continued the tradition of Mabel Dodge's affairs of a decade earlier and were a highlight of the New York social calendar.

Van Vechten had many friends and was warmly generous to them. In addition to maintaining a steady volume of correspondence with acquaintances in the United States and abroad, he loved to send gifts of books and records.[25] He sent copies of his own books to Fitzgerald and Maugham, exchanged publications with his close friend James Weldon Johnson, and recommended a variety of current titles to his correspondents. Van Vechten also bought multiple copies of his favorite records to give to acquaintances as distant as the young expatriate Man Ray in Paris.

The controversy over his Harlem book did not deter Van Vechten from spending the remainder of the 1920s in a whirlwind of travel and entertainment. He also did some writing. *Spider Boy*, his sixth novel, was inspired by an extended visit to Hollywood. It appeared in 1928 to lukewarm reviews and moderate sales. His final novel, *Parties*, was begun two weeks after the catastrophic stock market crash of 1929 and published in 1930. This amusing but ultimately tragic work served as a bittersweet epitaph for both the "spendid drunken twenties" and Van Vechten's career as a novelist. The book's insights on the vanished culture of plenty were lost on Depression America. It received several savage reviews and sold poorly.

ⴰⴰⴰⴰⴰⴰⴰⴰⴰⴰⴰ

While Van Vechten knew that the time for his fiction had passed, this realization caused no heartache. Royalties from his earlier books had accumulated impressively, and the inheritance of one million dollars in trust from the estate of his brother moved Van Vechten from a condition of financial comfort to one of distinct privilege. Liberated from all commercial concerns, he was free to do whatever he liked. To conclude his career as a writer, Van Vechten prepared his final book, a retrospective collection of largely auto-biographical essays titled *Sacred and Profane Memories*. Then, at the age of fifty-one, he turned to an entirely new endeavor.

By the middle of February 1932, before the official publication of his final book, Van Vechten had become a photographer. While this decision was triggered by his introduction to the Leica camera, Van Vechten had long been fascinated by the medium. He had collected photographs of theater stars as a child, and had been an avid amateur photographer in his adolescence. Years later, in reminiscing on this aspect of his career, Van Vechten stated that he had "always been interested in photographs and photography, other people's as well as my own."[26]

Although photography had been in use for forty years before Van Vechten's birth, he was a member of the first generation to consider the process a truly ubiquitous part of modern life. The medium had been introduced in late 1839 in the form of the daguerreotype, a process of magical clarity and recalcitrant difficulty. The relative expense and one-of-a-kind nature of the daguerreotype caused it to be replaced in the late 1850s by the wet-collodion glass-plate negative and paper print processes. This technology allowed photographs to be generated in quantity and a popular market arose for mass-produced celebrity portraits and scenic views.[27] The cumbersome and finicky wet-collodion process dominated the practice of photography for three decades before itself being superseded in the early 1880s by increasingly sensitive dry emulsions. The introduction only a few years later of flexible films and the hand camera combined to liberate photography forever from the exclusive domain of the professional and serious amateur. Middle- and upper-class Americans now became the producers, as well as the consumers, of photographs.

By the time of Van Vechten's youth the making of "snapshots" had become remarkably easy. Encouraged by George Eastman's advertising for the Kodak camera—"You Press the Button—We Do the Rest"—photography became a widely popular hobby. By the 1890s amateur photographers of all ages were able to record public events as well as the most casual and ephemeral moments of everyday life. It was also at this time that advances in printing allowed the inexpensive reproduction of photographs in newspapers and books by the halftone process. The result of these innovations was a geometric increase in the production and dissemination of photographically derived images. These changes lie at the root of our own image-saturated culture a century later.

Van Vechten began taking photographs in about 1895 at the age of fifteen. Not surprisingly, these earliest images depict his family, friends, and surroundings in Cedar Rapids. Using a simple box camera, he recorded his parents and grandmother, the Van Vechten house in winter

2   *Circus Parade in Cedar Rapids*, ca. 1895

3   *[Neighborhood girls] in* Egypta, *Cedar Rapids*, ca. 1895

and summer, neighbors sitting on front porches, and a circus parade in the center of town (figure 2). His interest in theater is revealed in playful outdoor tableaux of female classmates posed as vaudeville performers or parodying scenes from popular dramas (figure 3). Van Vechten also took his camera on vacation trips to Michigan and Ohio. He printed some of these negatives himself on the blue-toned cyanotype paper commonly used by amateurs of the period.

Van Vechten continued making snapshots after he left Cedar Rapids. During his college years in Chicago he recorded fellow students, nattily dressed and in high spirits, on their way into the city. Van Vechten's documents of his dorm room suggest his tastes and interests: literary posters filled the walls, while his desk and dresser were covered with framed photographs of family and friends. The self-reflexive impulse at the heart of Van Vechten's work is also suggested in a snapshot made during his tenure with the *American*. It depicts a friend beside a poster that reads: "Most Famous Novelists, Sketch Writers,

Literary Leaders of the West Write of the News in the CHICAGO AMERICAN."

After his move to New York, Van Vechten made similar photographic documents of people and places of special interest. In 1907, on his first trip to Europe, he photographed in Paris, Munich, and London. It was in this period that he made his first documentary images of artists, using his simple Kodak to record opera singers he had interviewed for the *New York Times*: Luisa Tetrazzini on the street in New York, for example, and Olive Fremstad in Paris. In the 1920s he also frequently sat for portraits by such respected New York photographers as E.O. Hoppé and Nickolas Muray (figure 4), and was able to study their working methods first hand.[28]

Clues to Van Vechten's interest in photography and its leading practitioners are sprinkled throughout his novels. In his first book a portrait by Hoppé is mentioned, and one of the characters praises the photographs of Alfred Stieglitz and Baron Adolph de Meyer.[29] In *Spider Boy*, the celebrity of the protagonist is indicated by the fact that he had been photographed by Edward Steichen for *Vanity Fair*. Such references underscore Van Vechten's appreciation of photography as a vehicle of both personal artistic expression and popular myth-making on a grand scale. For Van Vechten an important attribute of fame was the abiding presence of the camera with all its associations of glamour and energy: the press of reporters and the dramatic popping of flash bulbs.

Complex issues of representation lie just below the surface of Van Vechten's writing. His work suggests that identity is at once captured and invented by the camera, and that this process of self-reflection is central to any understanding of the modern self. His extensive series of self-portraits underscores this concern (frontispiece; figure 5). To avoid the camera is, somehow, to be less than fully real: the elusiveness of the central figure of Van Vechten's first novel is exemplified by the fact that he was never photographed.[30] The camera objectively collects fragments of visual experience at the same time that it blurs the meaning of reality by filling the world with simulations. At a Hollywood party a Van Vechten character muses that "some of the men were extremely handsome, at least as handsome as the models who posed to advertise golf clothes," unsure whether those he saw were, in fact, the same people recorded in such advertisements or merely fashionable types imitating these idealized images.[31]

Van Vechten also explored this tension between truth and invention by including a number of photographic illustrations in a revised 1927 edition of *Peter Whiffle*. Images of several subjects mentioned in the book, including at least one of Van Vechten's own snapshots of a Paris cafe, lent a curious authenticity to the fictional text. However, this inclusion only

4   Nickolas Muray: *Carl Van Vechten and Fania Marinoff*, July 5, 1923

5   *Self-Portrait*, September 5, 1933

emphasized that even the most improbable of his stories rested on a foundation of clear visual description.

Van Vechten's interest in photography was magnified a hundred fold in early February 1932. His friend Miguel Covarrubias had just returned from Europe with a new Leica camera and Van Vechten was fascinated by it. The Leica was both beautifully crafted and remarkably small (figure 1). The first "miniature" camera designed to use inexpensive 35mm film (spooled lengths of standard motion picture stock), the Leica changed both the practice and aesthetic of photography. Amateurs and professionals alike accepted the slightly granular look of prints made from these small negatives in exchange for the camera's unmatched ease of handling. Photojournalists gradually overcame their prejudice in favor of larger formats to embrace the rapid-fire ability of the 35mm, while artists such as Henri Cartier-Bresson used the fast and inconspicuous camera to make a pioneering series of surrealistic street pictures in the early 1930s.[32]

Excited by the enormous potential of the Leica, Van Vechten promptly bought one for himself and "immediately decided to regard photography seriously."[33] Despite the camera's ease of operation, however, there were innumerable technical difficulties to overcome. An early attempt to use artificial lights resulted in blown fuses throughout his apartment. Van Vechten was even more dismayed to find that his first formal portrait session, with the Chinese-American actress Anna May Wong, had mystifyingly resulted in a "perfectly blank" roll of film.[34] However, through trial and error, as well as advice from some of the most noted professionals of his day, Van Vechten became proficient with the medium.[35]

While the challenges of photography were very real for Van Vechten, particularly in the early stages of his work, he felt overwhelmed by the medium's potentials. As he later wrote,

> Photography is the most exigent of mistresses, both demanding and rewarding, depending on the amount of success achieved. It becomes an addiction (even an affliction) or an enchantment. Endless time and patience are prerequisites, and important results imply persistent research, considerable experiment, a fabulous amount of trial, with acceptance or rejection of the results. However, it is probably the most fascinating of the arts, if it is an art, and the more time spent on understanding its possibilities and its limitations, the more brilliant are the consequences.[36]

By the end of May 1932 he had a complete darkroom in his apartment and was soon doing all his own film processing and print developing.[37] Van Vechten quickly established a routine of beginning in the darkroom early in the morning and working for hours at a time. While many photographers find these tasks tedious, Van Vechten enjoyed them immensely.

> Developing and printing are much the most fascinating parts of photography because...you have to do things in

a very skillful way and depend entirely on yourself. When you're taking pictures, you depend somewhat on the subject, and if you have an assistant, which I have, he does the lighting. But developing and printing are fascinating, [and by] far the most interesting side of photography.[38]

Van Vechten became skilled at this work and, although never the most finicky purist, applied considerable thought to the print-making process.[39] The thousands of prints that issued from Van Vechten's darkroom over the next three decades were all made by his hand. However, he was not reluctant to enlist a series of close friends (including Donald Angus, Prentiss Taylor, Mark Lutz, and Saul Mauriber) to help with lighting and other tasks.

Over the years Van Vechten would produce thousands of pictures of architecture, street activity, and a variety of other subjects (figures 6, 7). His most focused interest, however, was portraiture.[40] His first sitters, not unexpectedly, were close acquaintances. In the first two months of his photography he recorded friends from Harlem such as James Weldon Johnson, Langston Hughes, and Paul Robeson (plate 3), as well as such literary and musical figures as Eugene O'Neill and Aaron Copland. Within the first few weeks of this work Van Vechten was also able to photograph personalities he admired, but did not personally know, such as the Mexican painter Frida Kahlo (plate 5). While simple in technique and composition, these initial images convey great warmth and vitality.

His mania for collecting and cataloging, in concert with his boundless passion for the medium, led Van Vechten quickly to realize that his aims in photography transcended the casual recording of a few notable friends. It became clear to him, in fact, that his goal was to construct a visual register of the leading creative talents of his time.[41] This was absurdly ambitious, of course, and not "objectively" possible by any standard. However, Van Vechten had little interest in Platonic notions of a neutral and scientific sort of objectivity. He celebrated cataloging, in large measure, as a subjective activity that reflected the personality of the compiler at least as much as the impersonal facts of the world.

By its nature, photography lends itself to the production and accumulation of precise visual data. The ease of the process permits the creation of images in great quantity. The factual density of photographs–their ability to record myriad details in a consistent and decipherable way–makes them ideal for both the documentation of unique subjects and the comparison and contrast of any quantity of such subjects.

From the beginning of its history a number of photographers have utilized this dual documentary function to produce personal, encyclopedic collections of various kinds. In this century the works of Eugene Atget (1857-1927) and August Sander (1876-1964) are best known. The former artist devoted thirty years to creating a monumental and richly poetic visual catalog of Paris and its environs. Collectively, Atget's thousands of views of storefronts, streets, parks, and people constitute a personal vision of the meaning of French culture.[42] While he focused exclusively on portraiture, August Sander's approach was equally ambitious. Working in Germany in the years between the world wars, he labored on a self-initiated project to document the people of his time. He recorded individuals from all occupations and walks of life–from farmers and teachers to bakers, businessmen, and beggars–before his work was ended by Nazi repression.[43]

Van Vechten certainly lacked some measure of Atget's and Sander's genius for visual invention. However, in addition to their uncommon persis-

6   *Polar Bears Bathing on Hot Day, Prospect Park, Brooklyn,* July 25, 1938

7   *At the Newsstand, Barcelona,* June 13, 1935

tence, all shared a belief that personal expression could be achieved through the accumulated visual evidence of their own time and place. All three bodies of work are prodigious in size and combine the intentions of artist, preservationist, and historian. Each celebrates the complexity of culture, the beauty of precisely transcribed facts, and the importance of memory. In addition, each weaves fact and opinion seamlessly together. Van Vechten's work, like that of Atget and Sander, is both a useful document of selected aspects of his time and a richly articulated self portrait. Van Vechten's ideas, interests, and physical presence define the nature of his photographic vision just as they permeate his criticism and fiction.

While Van Vechten's photographic archive grew steadily in magnitude, it inevitably remained partial in both scope and vision. However, the strength of this collection stemmed precisely from Van Vechten's own biases. The frequency of black faces in his grand portrait collection, for example, reflected his deep interest in African-American culture. No other white photographer of this period devoted anything approaching Van Vechten's energy to the sympathetic portrayal of black writers and artists. It seems apparent, in fact, that his work constitutes the single most integrated photographic vision of American arts and letters produced in his era. While standard practice today, this celebration of cultural diversity was most unusual sixty years ago. Similarly, Van Vechten's extensive documentation of contemporary dance stemmed from his long-standing interest in the subject.[44]

To a significant degree, the uniqueness of Van Vechten's work reflected his status as an amateur. He admired many of the leading commercial photographers of his day but had no need or desire to enter their profession. As an amateur– or, as some would have it, a dilettante–Van Vechten had the freedom to spend his time strictly as he pleased. In addition to its practical benefits, this status carried symbolic meaning. Many aesthetes valued nonprofessionalism as an important sign of artistic integrity. Classic dandies such as Lord Byron and Aubrey

Beardsley had been so far removed from the mundane world of labor that no one ever saw them at work.[45] The art photography movement of the early twentieth century, exemplified by the career of Alfred Stieglitz, continued part of this tradition by rejecting all thought of commerce. Only if artists were free from the marketplace, it was believed, could they pursue higher and purer motives. Of course, few were troubled by the fact that only those already financially secure could afford to hold such exalted ideals.

Despite his nonprofessional status, Van Vechten's work reflected significant aspects of the leading commercial photography of his day. He knew very well the work of men such as Baron Adolph de Meyer, Nickolas Muray, Cecil Beaton, George Hoyningen-Huene, and Edward Steichen.[46] Each issue of *Vogue* and *Vanity Fair* included images by photographers such as these, and the stylistic vocabulary of their work was widely influential. In addition to weaving elements of their style into his own, Van Vechten photographed many of the same subjects.[47] All these photographers traveled in sophisticated circles and their work reflected an easy familiarity with the realms of art, theater, fashion, film, and wealth. The celebrity portraiture that resulted was flattering, visually inventive, and opulently artificial. The goal of this work was to bring each subject to life, or, if it could be done, to something considerably larger than life.

While Van Vechten's style embodied important elements of this refined commercial aesthetic it also differed in significant ways. Due in part to his much simpler working method, Van Vechten's photographs are generally less complex in visual effect than those produced in the best-equipped studios of the day. For example, the noted commercial photographer Grancel Fitz depicted George Gershwin within a carefully choreographed, angular, jazz-age composition (figure 8). By contrast, Van Vechten's portrait of the popular composer is restrained and intimate (plate 14), suggesting his warmth as a person more than the modernity of his music.

The relative naturalism of Van Vechten's style resulted in a more literal and immediate vision than that of some of his most inventive peers. For example, he never employed the intricate staging, charged surrealism, and provocative sexuality of his young acquaintance George Platt Lynes (figure 9).[48] He also did not attempt to emulate the polished stylization of some of Edward Steichen's images. Steichen's highly reductive portrait of Anna May Wong depicts only the actress's head, with eyes closed, in tandem with a single chrysanthemum blossom on a darkly reflective glass surface.[49] The result is abstract and static: the subject as an elegant, Brancusi-like work of sculpture. While equally sophisticated in feeling, Van Vechten's portrait of the actress creates a far more dynamic sense of seduction and mystery (plate 1). Depicted in tight close-up, Wong stares coolly at the camera while sipping champagne. This image blends a sense of formal elegance with hints of a spectrum of licentious pleasures. While Van Vechten embraced the artificiality and control of the studio environment, his interest remained focused on the physical reality–the living, breathing presence–of his subjects.

Van Vechten's choice of camera also set him apart from the professional practice of his day. The standard tool for studio photographers was the 8 x 10-inch view camera, which produced minutely detailed negatives and prints of crystalline elegance. The Leica, by contrast, was considered a camera for amateurs or photojournalists, best suited to rapid outdoor action and a more immediate, grittier vision. Van Vechten's

9   George Platt Lynes: *Paul Cadmus*, 1941

8   W. Grancel Fitz: *George Gershwin*, 1929

choice of the Leica was based to a large degree on its technical simplicity, but he fully understood its inherent aesthetic. As a result, his photographs combine the control and artificiality of the studio environment with the more spontaneous vision of the snapshot or journalistic document. This synthesis was very unusual at the time. In hindsight it seems clear that Van Vechten's approach represented an early expression of a newly realist style in American commercial work. Martin Munkacsi, who wrote in 1935 that "all great photographs today are snapshots," is the photographer generally credited with pioneering this stylistic change.[50]

Van Vechten's new interest naturally brought him into increased contact with the leading photographers of his day. Berenice Abbott, Nickolas Muray, Doris Ulmann, Margaret Bourke-White, Alfred Stieglitz, George Hoyningen-Huene, Henri Cartier-Bresson, and Cecil Beaton all came to his apartment studio to pose, and on one of his visits to Paris, Van Vechten made several images of the noted painter and photographer Man Ray (figures 10, 11; plate 31). Van Vechten also shared his enthusiasm for photography with friends–including George Gershwin, Eugene O'Neill, and W. Somerset Maugham–who held an amateur's interest in the medium.

Once established in his makeshift apartment studio, Van Vechten used his considerable charm to entice friends and acquaintances to pose for him. He also used a variety of personal contacts to lure other noted subjects before his camera. His wife, actress Fania Marinoff, had many friends in the theater world, while Alfred A. Knopf, his publisher, provided introductions to a number of renowned authors. Acquaintances from a variety of other disciplines gladly made inquiries on Van Vechten's behalf, and his log of sitters grew steadily. Van Vechten's circle of associates was so extensive that he almost always found some entrée to any subject that interested him.[51]

The photographic sessions in Van Vechten's apartment studio were often elaborate affairs. He kept an extensive collection of props, clothing, furniture, and backdrops on hand to ensure that each sitter would be treated in a suitably unique and expressive manner. As his subject assumed the designated pose, Van Vechten readied his tripod-mounted Leica and instructed his assistant in the placement of lights. He then began to work, making one exposure after another, with frequent pauses for changes in pose, costume, lighting, and backdrop.

The often lively backgrounds Van Vechten used for his portraits were very carefully considered. The idea for them had been borrowed from the paintings of Matisse, and they became an important element of Van Vechten's style.[52] He acquired numerous rolls of fabric and patterned paper, and spent considerable effort selecting backdrops that evoked the character or mood of his subject. For patriotic composer George M. Cohan (plate 15), for example, a stars and stripes motif was used. Cab Calloway was recorded before a topical reference to the repeal of prohibition (plate 16). Charles Henri Ford (plate 25) and Ethel Waters (plate 35) were depicted with backgrounds echoing designs in their clothing, suggesting, respectively, a tense introversion and a gentle grace.

In other instances Van Vechten used simple backdrops with equal success. The minimal pattern behind Anna May Wong (plate 1) perfectly sets off the high elegance of her attire and pose. Backgrounds of pure black and white seem appropriate for Van Vechten's images of Katharine Cornell (plate 10) and Marsden Hartley (plate 32). Similarly, his powerful portrait of Billie Holiday (plate 51) draws great strength from the parallel between her world-weary expression and almost painfully unadorned surroundings. Van Vechten could also be surprisingly clever in his use of simple backdrops of draped fabric. In his portrait of Marlon Brando (plate 46), for example, the languid folds of the background material suggest a magnified detail of Brando's jacket.

Van Vechten was also highly conscious of the effects and potentials of lighting. In particular, he was interested in the use of shadow for both formal and expressive effect. His fascination for the evocative power of shadows is suggested in the musings of a character in *The Blind Bow-Boy*:

> She remembered how some one had said of her that she was like a pleasant pool...exposing a dormant silvery surface...or rippling placidly...with shadows, which portended hidden depths. No one, she reflected, save herself, knew how deep the pool was, or what might lie

10   *Doris Ulmann*, April 24, 1933

11   *Alfred Stieglitz*, April 17, 1935

concealed at the bottom... Shadows! There must be a philosophy of shadows! Shadows were the only realities. And there were always shadows, but most people overlooked the shadow in their search for the object which cast it.[53]

On some level Van Vechten's photography represented an intuitive attempt to outline a visual "philosophy of shadows" and to explore their expressive potential. He was interested in two levels of representation: the glamorous or public "silvery surface" of his subjects, and the "hidden depths" of their personalities. The frequent darkness of his prints–the use of deep velvety tones or even impenetrable shadow for graphic and emotional effect–suggests his fascination for inner states that could only be implied indirectly.

Van Vechten utilized shadows and dark tonalities in a variety of evocative ways. In his tautly constructed portrait of Bill Robinson (plate 6), Van Vechten cleverly used a shadow on the background fabric to echo the tilt of his subject's head. He charged his portrait of Thomas Wolfe with melodrama and foreboding by including Wolfe's own distorted shadow as an important part of the scene (plate 41). In an image of Truman Capote, Van Vechten deliberately let shadows play over his subject's youthful face (plate 45). The result–in combination with the background marionettes–conveys a sense of submerged mystery that a more traditional lighting arrangement would not have suggested. Compare this image, for example, with another from the same session (figure 12) suggesting a very different aspect of Capote's character.

In a significant percentage of his other works Van Vechten literally immersed his subjects in shadow. In a few cases the head of his sitter is recorded looming out of a solid rectangle of inky blackness, creating a sense of both isolation and proud self-sufficiency (plates 9, 10). In many other instances (for example, plates 7, 8, 13, 14, 21, 22) shadows are integrated with background elements but strongly dominate both the composition and mood of the photograph.

Van Vechten's repeated use of shadows suggests his interest in the shaded depths of psychology. Paradoxically, however, he also valued profoundly the expressive richness of the clearly described surface. Although his pictures contain a variety of formal ideas, Van Vechten often recorded his subjects simply and directly in head-and-shoulders compositions. This straightforward approach allowed him to focus on what was tangible and visible: textures of clothing, the strength of a glance, and the myriad details of body language and gesture.

This aspect of Van Vechten's working method finds an echo in a passage from Italo Calvino's *Difficult Loves*. Calvino's fictional photographer, dismayed by the "quicksands of moods, humors, [and] psychology," decides to aim instead

> at a portrait completely on the surface, evident, unequivocal, that did not elude conventional appearance, the stereotype, the mask. The mask, being first of all a social, historical product, contains more truth than any image claiming to be "true"; it bears a quantity of meanings that will gradually be revealed.[54]

The mask, as both Baudelaire and Van Vechten would have agreed, did indeed reveal far more than it concealed. The conventions of dress, expression, and pose all spoke of larger–and often relatively invisible–influences and motives. These conventions suggested both the source of individual traits and universal patterns of behavior.

The duality between inner reality and outer appearances–what we "are" and the masks we wear–lies at the heart of both Van Vechten's portraiture and our complex modern notions of

12   *Truman Capote*, March 30, 1948

identity. As Leo Braudy has observed, ideas of celebrity and selfhood are intimately connected: "...the history of fame is inseparable from the history of human self-consciousness, on the part of both the aspirant and the audience."[55] It may be suggested that Van Vechten's thousands of portraits represent an extended meditation on the meaning of celebrity in a democratic society, and the elusiveness of fixed ideas of the self.

Modern notions of fame arose in the nineteenth century in cultures in which egalitarian ideas were challenging or supplanting systems of inherited prestige. In these societies it was possible through talent, education, and personal will to transcend boundaries of experience previously defined by birth status alone. Achievement became a product of individual ability and initiative, with fame and social mobility closely allied. Correspondingly, the uniqueness of the self and the value of self-expression were increasingly celebrated. With systems of inherited status weakened, greater attention was paid to the variety of "selves" that seemed possible.

In America these ideas were linked in enormously complex ways with the rise of show business and the mass media. Vaudeville, theater, and the circus in the nineteenth century, and radio and film in the early twentieth, were all about public performance and role-playing. By the 1920s a significant shift was well under way. Most of the celebrities of an earlier era had been people of lineage and property, or leaders in political, military, and economic affairs. They represented cultural hierarchies and networks of power and influence. However, the new celebrities of the era of film and the tabloid press were more often drawn from the fields of art and entertainment.[56] These individuals were celebrated for the uniqueness of their talents and the appeal of their public persona. Newspaper reporters (like Van Vechten in his early career) and photographers served the important function of mediating between celebrities and a mass public eager to find some reflection of itself in these increasingly larger-than-life figures.

There was a profound theatricality in the conventions of these genres and in the images of fame created and promulgated by the media. To be famous was to be both more and less "real" than ordinary people. Superficial qualities became familar to a public of millions, while any larger sense of individuality was suppressed to conform to some generic role in "the audience's continuing drama of the meaning of human nature."[57] Viewers required of celebrities certain signs of uniqueness and authenticity, but these were accepted only when drawn from a very narrow range of options.

This complex involvement with images and icons of the self, and an awareness of role-playing and theatricality, permeated the intellectual realms of American culture. The rituals of daily life, and the work of artists who emphasized the conventions of their disciplines (Luigi Pirandello and Bertolt Brecht in theater, for example), all were examined with new interest.[58] While certainly not a leader in this aspect of modernist thought, Van Vechten's work embodies intriguing aspects of these concepts in a uniquely personal way.

Van Vechten's photographs reflect a complexity of influences and ideas. On their simplest level, they are images of talented people made by a midwesterner who never lost his childhood fascination for the glamour of celebrity and the liberating power of art. These photographs stem from the same impulse that motivated him to collect portraits of theater personalities in his youth, and to keep a guest book for the autographs of visitors until the end of his life. Van Vechten remained eternally "star-struck," and his photographs, in many ways, are about the aura and manifestations of fame.

Van Vechten's pictures are also very clearly about style: his own style as an artist, and the tastes and temperaments of his subjects. As such, his images prod the viewer to think about the importance of aesthetic concerns in shaping our understanding of both the world and ourselves. The undisguised nature of Van Vechten's props and the frequent theatricality of his poses–the most obvious devices of his style–remind us of the constructed nature of all such representations.

Thoughtful study of these portraits suggests the tension between presence and presentation, and the process by which photographer and subject collaborate to create a likeness. Most of Van Vechten's sitters were public figures, and thus accustomed to being photographed. Van Vechten himself had considerable experience on both sides of the camera. As a result, his images often suggest a canny dialogue between celebrities with great skills of self-presentation and a photographer who understood–and was fascinated by–those abilities. Van Vechten's portraits are usually flattering while at the same time reminding us of the desire of every sitter (including Van Vechten himself) to be flattered.

Van Vechten made many exposures of his subjects. Individual portrait sessions often produced several dozen carefully considered frames recording evidence of numerous costume changes and repositioning of lights and props. Some of his closest subjects were recorded year after year. This interest in compiling variant interpretations of individual sitters suggests that Van Vechten viewed identity as multifaceted and plastic. Each camera portrait represents a split-second vision of a continuous and complex dynamic between the subject's efforts to compose a presentation "self" and the photographer's interpretive abilities. Van Vechten made many exposures in order to explore, as fully as he could, both the visual potential of his sitters and the range of his own interpretive ideas.

These ideas were evoked in particularly complex form in the images that are at once Van Vechten's most overtly theatrical and his most documentary: his portraits of actors posed in simulations of stage roles (plates 43, 46, 47, and 48). Issues of identity, role-playing, celebrity, and fabrication are all rolled deliciously together in these photographs. We perceive the subjects as both themselves and their characters, and interpret each pose as an attempt to project an "authentic" image of a well-practiced artifice. These paradoxes are emblematic of Van Vechten's own synthesis of documentary and interpretive concerns, and his abiding fascination for the masks of fame and the constructed nature of identity. These pictures also serve as introductions to the dizzying complexity of modern notions of representation and the self.

One cannot be certain how apparent, or relevant, these concepts were to viewers in the 1930s and 1940s. Interpretations of the past are inevitably influenced by the values and tastes of the present, and the intellectual climate of the 1990s certainly places greater emphasis–or at least a more focused kind of emphasis–on issues of identity and theatricality. It remains clear, however, that these ideas were integral to Van Vechten's expressive vision. They are, in fact, what give his work an artistic dimension beyond the simply documentary.

In late 1935 Van Vechten's portraits were shown in the Second International Leica Exhibition along with works by such celebrated photographers as Cecil Beaton, George Platt Lynes, Man Ray, and Edward Steichen.[59] In his review of this exhibit the critic Henry McBride praised Van Vechten's work by noting that "what is literature's loss is photography's gain–quite distinctly Mr. Van Vechten is the Bronzino of this camera age."[60] The comparison was apt. Agnolo Bronzino (1503-1572) was the quintessential High Mannerist artist in Florence. He was particularly noted for his court portraits, which conveyed the high status of his subjects through detailed depictions of costume and the evocation of a detached, self-assured superiority. Bronzino used a clearly defined set of representational conventions to reinforce and celebrate the high station of his sitters.

This reference suggests a useful art-historical context for Van Vechten's work. His portrait photographs may be best understood on a continuum between Bronzino and Andy Warhol. All three of these artists employed a mannered style to flatter their subjects while consciously exploring (and perhaps exploiting) larger cultural ideas on the meaning of the self and its representations. All were acutely aware of the art of their time, and their styles reflect self-conscious manipulations of its conventions.

The differences in their visions suggest important shifts in western thought and culture. Bronzino's lustrous subjects were notable for their lineage and political and economic power. In his paintings the members of the Venetian court were depicted as unquestionably superior and serenely self-assured. Van Vechten's work, on the other hand, surveys an aesthetic aristocracy. His pantheon of artists and performers was founded on a Romantic faith in the value of individual expression and flourished in the (relatively) egalitarian climate and nascent mass communications of mid-twentieth-century America. Van Vechten's subjects are at once mortal and larger than life, and this tension animates his work.

Warhol's celebrity images of the 1960s emphasize the distancing effect of media representations.[61] His silkscreened paintings of Marilyn and Elvis are deliberately flattened, disembodied, and abstracted. Such works suggest that no "real" Marilyn Monroe or Elvis Presley exists or, more precisely, that former links between some "genuine" self and one's public persona have been severed. In Warhol's rather joyless celebration of fame the only reality is a ghostly image, repeated endlessly and sustained by the dreams and projections of an anonymous public.

Van Vechten's photographs contain hints of Warhol's themes, but his vision is ultimately far more optimistic. Van Vechten's subjects are understood to be willing participants in the creation of their media personas. They collaborate with the photographer as active, willful beings at once open, and resistant, to interpretation. While skilled at the creation of public "selves," these subjects remain flesh-and-blood individuals. The result is a dynamic balance of synthetic image and physical reality, with the former not threatening to replace or destroy the latter.

While Warhol practiced a stance of cool indifference–the artist as insatiable machine eye–Van Vechten's pictures evoke his enthusiasm for both his subjects and his medium. For him, photography was a very "warm" medium, with each portrait the product of a close physical and intellectual interaction. Van Vechten loved the intensity and relative intimacy of the process. Late in life he expressed the meaning photography had come to hold for him.

> Photography's a very personal thing. It's magical, too....I used to be continually surprised by people that had very even features turning out to be very ugly in photography. It has something to do with how alive they are. Many people who have these very even features look dead in photographs, because they haven't any vitality to show. If your subject shows vitality in photographs, you are usually on your way to success. I know that now, in a way, so that I can help people to achieve vitality...you can stir them up; you can annoy them. You can make them feel.[62]

Van Vechten's photographs remain interesting because they are full of conceptual and pictorial vitality. They reflect deeply complex issues of identity and celebrity, as well as the feelings Van Vechten had for his subjects and his era. Van Vechten's life was one of uninhibited enthusiasms, and his photography a celebration of individual creativity and accomplishment. His pictures chronicle a generation of celebrities while reminding us of the visual vocabulary of fame. The best of his images combine historical and expressive intentions in a uniquely compelling way by consistently blurring the distinction between documentary and interpretive concerns. Van Vechten's success as a photographer ultimately reflects the fact that he observed the world he knew best with a wholly original combination of style and passion.

K. F. D.

Bibliographic Sources

The leading scholar on Van Vechten's life and work is unquestionably Bruce Kellner. In the preparation of this essay, the following works by Mr. Kellner were of invaluable assistance: *Carl Van Vechten and the Irreverent Decades* (Norman: University of Oklahoma Press, 1968); *"Keep A-Inchin' Along": Selected Writings of Carl Van Vechten about Black Arts and Letters* (Westport, Conn.: Greenwood Press, 1979); *A Bibligraphy of the Work of Carl Van Vechten* (Westport, Conn.: Greenwood Press, 1980); "Introduction," in *Carl Van Vechten: Vintage Photographs* (London: Duke Street Gallery, 1981); *Letters of Carl Van Vechten* (New Haven: Yale University Press, 1987); and *A Supplementary Bibliography of the Work of Carl Van Vechten* (privately published: 1991).

Also of great value were two fine volumes by Edward Lueders: *Carl Van Vechten and the Twenties* (Albuquerque: University of New Mexico Press, 1955); and *Carl Van Vechten* (New York: Twayne Publishers, 1965). Other secondary sources of note include: John D. Gordan, "Carl Van Vechten: Notes for an Exhibition in Honor of His Seventy-fifth Birthday," *Bulletin of the New York Public Library*, 59:7, July 1955, pp. 331-366; Paul Padgette, *The Dance Photography of Carl Van Vechten* (New York: Shirmer Books, 1981); Edward Burns, ed., *The Letters of Gertrude Stein and Carl Van Vechten, 1913-1946* (New York: Columbia University Press, 1986); and Van Vechten's own reminiscence of his photographic career, "Portraits of the Artists," *Esquire*, December 1962, pp. 170-174, 256-258.

Notes

1 Bruce Kellner, *Carl Van Vechten and the Irreverent Decades* (Norman: University of Oklahoma Press, 1968), p. 17.

2 *Carl Van Vechten and the Irreverent Decades*, p. 133.

3 Jonathan Mayne, ed., *The Painter of Modern Life and Other Essays by Charles Baudelaire* (New York: Da Capo Press, 1986), pp. 9, 17.

4 *The Painter of Modern Life*, pp. 26, 27.

5 Leo Braudy, *The Frenzy of Renown: Fame and Its History* (New York: Oxford University Press, 1986), p. 478.

6 *The Frenzy of Renown*, pp. 481-82.

7 *The Painter of Modern Life*, p. 28.

8 For a humorous overview of the aesthetic interests and affectations of Van Vechten's generation, see Ernest Boyd, "Aesthete: Model 1924," *The American Mercury*, 1:1, January, 1924, pp. 51-56.

9 For a most useful summary of the cultural significance of early twentieth-century nightlife in America, see Lewis A. Erenberg, *Steppin' Out: New York Nightlife and the Transformation of American Culture, 1890-1930* (Westport, Conn.: Greenwood Press, 1981).

10 *Carl Van Vechten and the Irreverent Decades*, p. 52.

11 *Carl Van Vechten and the Irreverent Decades*, p. 69.

12 Steven Watson, *Strange Bedfellows: The First American Avant-Garde* (New York: Abbeville Press, 1991), p. 136. For the flavor of these evenings, and Van Vechten's part in them, see pp. 129-138 of this volume.

13 *Strange Bedfellows*, p. 134.

14 Edward Lueders, *Carl Van Vechten* (New York: Twayne Publishers, 1965), p. 40.

15 *Strange Bedfellows*, p. 51.

16 Darryl Pinckney, "The Honorary Negro," *The New York Review of Books*, Aug. 18, 1988, p. 33.

17 Carl Van Vechten, *The Blind Bow-Boy* (New York: Alfred A. Knopf, 1923), pp. 16, 18. Gareth Brooks appears in *The Tattooed Countess* as a child, in *Firecrackers* as a world-weary snob, and in *Nigger Heaven* as an intellectual slummer in Harlem.

18 *Carl Van Vechten and the Irreverent Decades*, p. 143.

19 *Carl Van Vechten*, p. 59.

20 *The Blind Bow-Boy*, p. 160.

21 For a mid-century perspective on Van Vechten and his contemporaries, see William McFee, "Yesterday They Wrote Best Sellers," *The New York Times Book Review*, July 2, 1950.

22 "Nigger heaven" was used as a vernacular term for the balconies, to which blacks were usually relegated, of New York City motion picture theaters. With this application in mind, the phrase was also used by many Harlem residents to describe their neighborhood–as above, but largely invisible to, the white population of lower Manhattan.

23 The most balanced appraisal of *Nigger Heaven* is contained in Bruce Kellner's *"Keep A-Inchin' Along,"* pp. 3-15, and pp. 73-78. See also chapter 6, "Nigger Heaven," in David Levering Lewis, *When Harlem Was in Vogue* (New York: Oxford University Press, 1981).

24 *When Harlem Was in Vogue*, p. 183.

25 Van Vechten's penchant for correspondence was noted in 1951 by Eleanor Perényi ("Wanted: More Letters," *Vogue*, August 1, 1951): "A good letter is more personal than a telegram; it is more enduring than a phone call. Yet it is clear enough to most of us that letter-writing is in danger of passing out of our lives....I know of only one person who still has this charmingly old-fashioned habit–Carl Van Vechten, who sends cards to his friends with reminders that he is thinking about them, a suggestion that they read a book he has liked, or an invitation to tea. Since they come on post cards made from his own photographs, they provide a double gratification to his friends. He is a lone voice in the wilderness of a society founded on telephonic or telegraphic communication."

26 Letter of October 19, 1942, cited in Bruce Kellner, ed., *Letters of Carl Van Vechten* (New Haven: Yale University Press, 1987), p. 187.

27 For an introduction to the early history of "celebrity" photographs, see the chapter "Fame & Celebrity," in Vicki Goldberg's *The Power of Photography: How Photographs Changed Our Lives* (New York: Abbeville Press, 1991), pp. 103-133.

28 See Marianne Fulton Margolis, *Muray's Celebrity Portraits of the Twenties and Thirties* (New York: Dover Publications, 1978), plate 126.

29 In *Peter Whiffle* (New York: Alfred A. Knopf, 1922), p. 176, Edith Dale states that "Stieglitz and de Meyer put themselves in their cameras, that is why their photographs are wonderful..." The reference to E.O. Hoppé is on p. 194.

30 *Peter Whiffle*, p. 226.

31 *Spider Boy*, p. 91.

32 For an astute discussion of this work and the aesthetic potential of the hand camera, see Peter Galassi, *Henri Cartier-Bresson: The Early Work* (New York: Museum of Modern Art, 1987).

33 Carl Van Vechten, "Portraits of the Artists," *Esquire*, December, 1962, p. 174. This text, written by Van Vechten to accompany a portfolio of his portraits, is the best first-person summary of his background and experiences in photography.

34 *Letters of Carl Van Vechten*, p. 125.

35 In his 1962 *Esquire* essay Van Vechten notes: "I have known many of the great and well-known photographers and I have photographed a good many of them: the Baron de Meyer, Stieglitz, Steichen, Man Ray, Hoyningen-Huene, Cecil Beaton, Berenice Abbott, Henri Cartier-Bresson, Margaret Bourke-White, Nickolas Muray, Yousuf Karsh, [and] Richard Avedon. Some of these have given me valuable suggestions."

36 *Esquire*, December, 1962, p. 170.

37 Paul Padgette, in *The Dance Photography of Carl Van Vechten* (New York: Schirmer Books, 1981), p. 5, states that Van Vechten began developing his own film in May 1932, but had these negatives commercially printed until sometime in 1934. However, frequent references in his letters of the period suggest strongly that Van Vechten began making his own prints in May 1932, as soon as his darkroom was completed.

38 Excerpts from a 1960 interview with Van Vechten for the Columbia Oral History series. Quoted in *The Dance Photography of Carl Van Vechten*, p 5.

39 In his 1962 *Esquire* essay Van Vechten wrote: "I do not believe in cropping, even by myself." This apparently is a reference to his unwillingness to allow his photographs to be altered when reproduced in newspapers or magazines. However, some writers have assumed incorrectly that Van Vechten invariably (and rather simple-mindedly) printed the full frame of his negative. It is clear that he made an effort to compose his final picture at the time of exposure in order to make most efficient use of his small negatives. However, comparison of his original contact images (in the Van Vechten collection at Yale) with his enlarged exhibition prints reveals that he felt considerable freedom to crop his photographs if the composition could be improved. Such cropping ranges from minimal to quite significant and in every instance studied by the present writer resulted in a more powerful picture. This reveals a more active critical involvement in darkroom procedures than has previously been suggested.

40 In his *Esquire* essay Van Vechten wrote: "In the beginning I shot pictures at random, old buildings, groups in the street, trees in the park, or casual portraits of friends, but very soon I discovered that making portraits, serious portraits, would be my permanent aim." In addition to his steady work in the studio, Van Vechten photographed with some regularity on the New York streets and took his camera on most of his travels. A small sampling of the subjects of his city pictures includes: parades, objects at an outdoor market, signs, children, people walking or conversing, the El, window displays, the tall buildings of lower Manhattan, details of iron work and statues, and the Bronx Zoo. He produced a particularly large body of work–in both black and white and color–documenting pavilions and people at the 1939 New York World's Fair.

41 In looking back on his serious beginning in photography Van Vechten wrote in 1942: "I think it was my original intention to photograph everybody and everything in the world!" Cited in *Letters of Carl Van Vechten*, p. 187.

42 The most definitive work on Atget is *The Work of Atget*, a four volume set by John Szarkowski and Maria Morris Hambourg: *Volume One: Old France* (1981); *Volume Two: The Art of Old Paris* (1982); *Volume Three: The Ancien Regime* (1983); and *Volume Four: Modern Times* (1984); all published by the Museum of Modern Art, New York.

43 See August Sander, *Men Without Masks: Faces of Germany, 1910-1938* (Greenwich, Conn.: New York Graphic Society, 1973); and Gunther Sander, ed., *August Sander: Citizens of the Twentieth Century, Portrait Photographs 1892-1952* (Cambridge, Mass.: The MIT Press, 1989).

44 This aspect of Van Vechten's work is surveyed in *The Dance Photography of Carl Van Vechten*.

45 *The Frenzy of Renown*, p. 478. Similarly, a character in *The Blind Bow-Boy* (p. 161) describes successful art with these words: "It is amiable. It does not produce sweat. What is good is easy; everything divine runs with light feet..."

46 Monographs on all these photographers are available. For concise overviews of the celebrity portraiture of era, see Naomi Rosenblum, *A World History of Photography* (New York: Abbeville Press, 1984), pp. 495-499; and Nancy Hall-Duncan, *A History of Fashion Photography* (New York: Alpine Book Company, 1979), pp. 44-67.

47 For example, many of the subjects reproduced in this volume were also recorded by Edward Steichen. Steichen's portraits of Katharine Cornell, Lillian Gish, Paul Robeson, Anna May Wong, Eugene O'Neill, George M. Cohan, Thomas Mann, George Gershwin, Willa Cather, Charles Laughton, and H. L. Mencken are included in his *A Life in Photography* (Garden City, N.Y.: Doubleday & Company, 1963).

48 For background on Lynes's career, see Jack Woody, *George Platt Lynes Photographs 1931-1955* (Pasadena: Twelvetrees Press, 1981). Van Vechten's own homoerotic photographs–which he held discreetly private–were composed largely of rather chaste figure studies.

49 See *A Life in Photography*, p. 127.

50 Cited in Nancy White and John Esten, *Style In Motion: Munkacsi Photographs of the '20s, '30s, '40s* (New York: Clarkson N. Potter, 1979), np.

51 Of course, some desired subjects escaped him for reasons of scheduling or vanity. A few noted authors declined to pose for Van Vechten because they had little regard for his work. In other cases he was not able to establish appropriate contacts. At the end of 1936, for example, Van Vechten wanted to photograph Jesse Owens, the star of that summer's Olympic Games. He asked Bill Robinson, who knew Owens slightly, to try to arrange a sitting with the champion, but the attempt proved unsuccessful.

52 *Letters of Carl Van Vechten*, p. 187. In his 1962 *Esquire* piece Van Vechten stressed the influence of art on his photographic style. "I have known many great and celebrated painters and sculptors: Henri Matisse, Fernand Léger, Marie Laurencin, Marcel Duchamp, Raoul Dufy, Jacob Epstein, Rufino Tamayo, Georgia O'Keeffe, Louis Eilshemius, Giorgio di Chirico, Diego Rivera, Richmond Barthé, Charles Demuth, Marsden Hartley, Florine Stettheimer, Gaston Lachaise, [and] Antonio Salemme. I have photographed all these artists and have learned more from studying their work and the work of other painters and sculptors than I have from studying the work of other photographers."

53 *The Blind Bow-Boy* (New York: Alfred A. Knopf, 1923), p. 95. Ellipses in original.

54 Italo Calvino, *Difficult Loves*, trans. William Weaver (San Diego: Harcourt Brace Jovanovich, 1984), pp. 228-229. Cited in Jefferson Hunter, *Image and Word: The Interaction of Twentieth-Century Photographs and Texts* (Cambridge, Mass.: Harvard University Press, 1987), p. 115.

55 *The Frenzy of Renown*, p. 586. The following discussion owes much to the final section of this text, "Democratic Theater and the Natural Performer," pp. 450-598.

56 For a mid-century perspective on this subject, see C. Wright Mills, *The Power Elite* (New York: Oxford University Press, 1956), pp. 71-93.

57 *The Frenzy of Renown*, p. 589.

58 A useful introduction to these complex ideas is provided in Silvio Gaggi, *Modern/Postmodern: A Study in Twentieth-Century Arts and Ideas* (Philadelphia: University of Pennsylvania Press, 1989).

59 Van Vechten played a significant role in the next edition of this exhibit, held at Radio City from October 20 to November 2, 1936. Twelve of his pictures–a mixture of portraits and street scenes–were hung in the "professional" section of the show, and he was also one of four jurors (with Richard L. Simon, Anton Bruehl, and Manuel Komroff) who chose the recipients of the first and second prizes in each of three categories.

60 Quoted in *The Dance Photography of Carl Van Vechten*, p. 9.

61 For introductions to these themes, see, for example, David Bourdon, "Andy Warhol and the Society Icon," *Art in America*, January-February, 1975, pp. 42-45; and Robert Rosenblum, "Andy Warhol: Court Painter to the 70s," in *Andy Warhol: Portraits of the 70s*, David Whitney, ed., (New York: Whitney Museum of Art/Random House, 1979).

62 *The Dance Photography of Carl Van Vechten*, p. 6.

PLATES

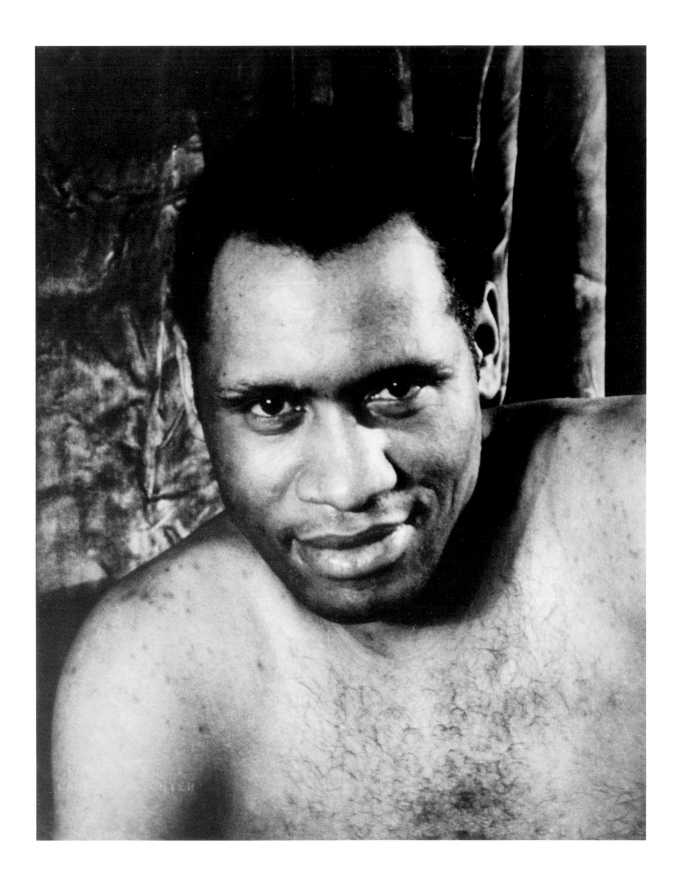

Gertrude Stein in her lecture robes, November 4, 1934

Bessie Smith, February 3, 1936

Lillian Gish, October 28, 1947

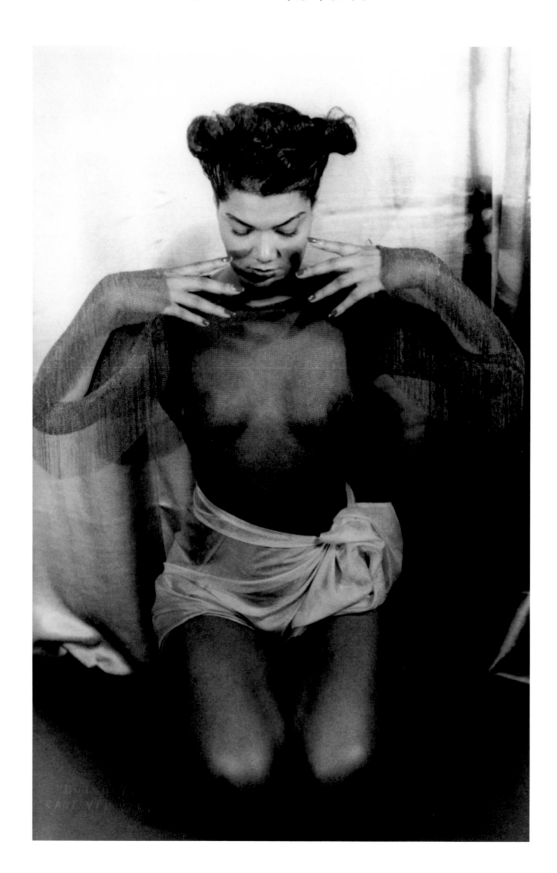

Pearl Bailey, July 5, 1946

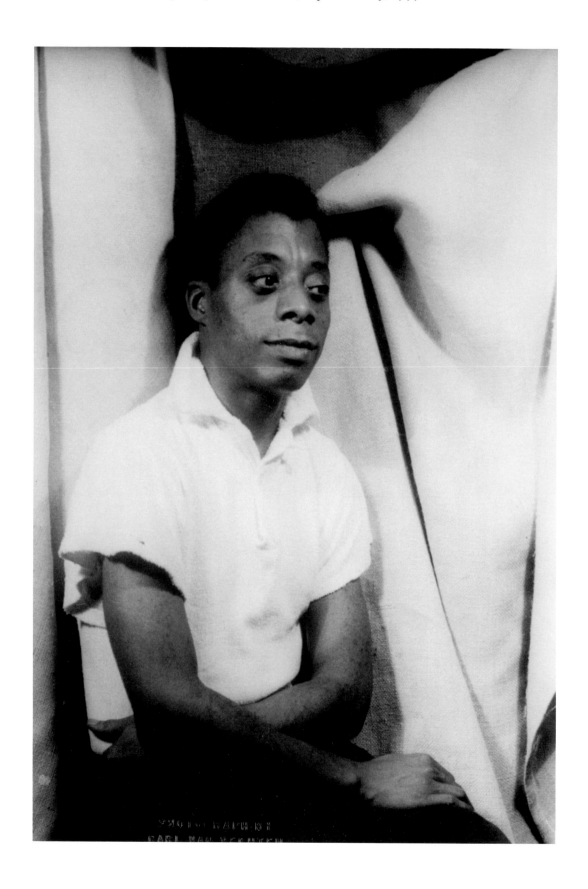

frontispiece *Self-Portrait*, March 9, 1934
  14" x 10½"
  Van Vechten's body of work includes a significant number of images of himself, many of which were made by friends using his camera. Others, including this image and figure 5, were identified by Van Vechten as his own work, and thus more clearly reflect his ideas about self-portrayal and pictorial composition.

1 *Anna May Wong*, April 20, 1932
  13⅞" x 11"
  The Chinese-American actress Anna May Wong (1907-1961) was a successful film star whose exotic beauty and lively humor endeared her to many. She began as a model in her native Los Angeles, and rose to stardom in *The Thief of Baghdad* (1924), a silent fantasy starring Douglas Fairbanks. In addition to playing roles in many American motion pictures, she worked in England, France, and Germany in the late 1920s. During this time she wrote and acted in a musical play, *Tschun-Tschi*, which was produced in Vienna. She returned to the United States in 1930 to resume her Hollywood career, and starred in a number of films in the next decade. She was comparatively inactive from the beginning of World War II until the late 1950s, when she attempted a comeback. Her final screen appearance was in *Portrait in Black* (1960), starring Lana Turner and Anthony Quinn.

2 *Georgette Harvey,* May 23, 1932
  14" x 11"
  Harvey (1883-1952) was a popular singer and character actress. Her quartet, The Creole Belles, performed in New York and Europe for sixteen years. After the dissolution of the group Harvey stayed in Europe, where she enjoyed considerable success. She lived in St. Petersburg for over a decade and was popular with members of Czar Nicholas's court. She fled the Russian revolution and eventually returned to New York, where she appeared regularly on the Broadway stage from 1930 through 1949. She earned particular praise for her performance in the original musical version of *Porgy and Bess* and its subsequent revivals.

3 *Paul Robeson,* March 7, 1932
  10" x 8"
  Robeson (1898-1976) was one of the finest actors and concert artists of his time. An excellent student, Robeson became only the third African-American to enter Rutgers College. He endured racial abuse with great dignity and graduated in 1919 as a champion athlete and class valedictorian. In 1920, during his studies at Columbia Law School, Robeson made his acting debut. In 1925 he gave an important solo concert at the Greenwich Village Theater in New York, and his fame as an actor and singer grew steadily in the United States and abroad. He was particularly noted for his stage roles in *Show Boat* (1928) and a British production of *Othello* (1930), and such films as *The Emperor Jones* (1933), *King Solomon's Mines* (1936), and *Jericho* (1937). Robeson was an eloquent spokesman for the causes of peace and racial understanding throughout his life.

4 *Claire Booth Brokaw [Luce],* December 9, 1932
  9" x 6⅝"
  Claire Booth Luce (1903-1987) was a playwright, politician, and celebrity. In the early 1930s she edited *Vogue* and *Vanity Fair* magazines, and wrote satirical articles for the latter. Between 1936 and 1939 she wrote three successful Broadway plays that were subsequently made into films. In 1935 she married publishing magnate Henry R. Luce. She served in the House of Representatives as a Republican from Connecticut between 1943 and 1947, and as Ambassador to Italy, 1953-1956. She was an amateur photographer in the years before her political career, and corresponded with Van Vechten on this subject.

5 *Frida Kahlo,* March 19, 1932
  14" x 11"
  The Mexican artist Frida Kahlo (1907-1954) was one of the most powerful and original painters of her time. Her work is full of emotion, anxiety, and painful self-revelation. She grew up during the time of the Mexican Revolution, a period of great interest in nationalistic themes and of political idealism. Kahlo was strongly influenced by these currents, and by her acquaintance with figures such as Tina Modotti, who introduced her to a sophisticated world of art and political activism. The nature of Kahlo's art stemmed in part from a near-fatal trolley accident in 1925 that left her handicapped. She began painting in 1926 and her physical and emotional problems provided the basis for her visceral work. She married the noted mural painter Diego Rivera in 1929, and accompanied him to the United States in 1930-33 during his work on various mural commissions. It was during one of these trips to New York that Van Vechten had the then little-known Kahlo pose in his studio. While Rivera's work has been consistently celebrated, Kahlo's own life and art only began receiving serious attention a quarter-century after her death.

6 *Bill Robinson,* January 25, 1933
  14" x 11"
  Bill "Bojangles" Robinson (1878-1949) was a celebrated dancer and star of Broadway musicals and Hollywood films. The grandson of a slave, he began tap dancing for pennies at the age of eight on the streets of Richmond, Virginia. He graduated to the vaudeville circuit and developed a broad following. The technique and originality of his soft-shoe and tap routines became widely celebrated and copied. Robinson began appearing in stage musicals in 1928 and in motion pictures in 1930. He is perhaps best remembered for his roles in four Shirley Temple films: *The*

Little Colonel (1935), *The Littlest Rebel* (1935), *Rebecca of Sunnybrook Farm* (1938), and *Just Around the Corner* (1938). His fourteen films also included *Harlem is Heaven* (1932), *In Old Kentucky* (1935), and the all-black musical *Stormy Weather* (1943). His nickname "Bojangles" became popularized after Fred Astaire's number of the same title in the 1936 *Swing Time,* and Sammy Davis, Jr.'s later hit record "Mr. Bojangles."

7 *Tallulah Bankhead,* January 25, 1934
137/8" x 103/4"

Bankhead (1903-1968) was born in Alabama to one of the state's most famous political families. After attending convent school she won a beauty contest and got a bit part in a Broadway play in 1918. Her first notable success came in Great Britain, where she worked from 1923 to 1930. She became a sensation in *The Dancers,* and young girls throughout England copied her clothes, hair, and speech. She returned to the United States in 1931 for films in Hollywood and stage appearances on Broadway. Her most notable success came in Lillian Hellman's drama *The Little Foxes* (1939), for which she received the New York Drama Critics' Circle award. Her film career included performances in *The Cheat* (1931), *Tarnished Lady* (1931), *The Devil and the Deep* (1932), *Thunder Below* (1932), *Faithless* (1932), *Lifeboat* (1944), *A Royal Scandal* (1945), and *Fanatic* (1964). She won a best acting award for *Lifeboat* from the New York Film Critics. She was perhaps more famous for her vibrant energy, sultry voice, and impetuous private life than for her acting skills.

8 *Judith Anderson,* September 28, 1932
133/8" x 11"

Dame Judith Anderson (1898-1992) was born in Adelaide, Australia, and made her stage debut in Sydney in 1915. She began working in New York in 1920. Her 1932 appearance as Lavinia in Eugene O'Neill's play *Mourning Becomes Electra* led to a long series of starring roles on both stage and screen. She was perhaps most highly praised for her role in Robinson Jeffers's *Medea.* Anderson and Van Vechten were good friends and he photographed her many times.

9 *James Weldon Johnson,* December 3, 1932
14" x 105/8"

Johnson (1871-1938) was one of the most influential African-American men of letters in the 1920s and 1930s. He was born into a middle-class family in Florida and received a degree from Atlanta University. While working as a high school principal he began writing poems and song lyrics. In 1902 he moved to New York, where he became increasingly involved in black and political causes. After becoming a staff member of the NAACP in 1916, Johnson traveled across the country to lecture on its behalf and to organize new chapters. His first book, *The Autobiography of an Ex-Colored Man* (1912), prompted

little attention, but his inspirational poem "Fifty Years" (1913), commemorating the anniversary of the Emancipation Proclamation, received widespread praise. His later publications included *Black Manhattan* (1930) and *Along This Way* (1933). Van Vechten met Johnson in 1924 and they became close friends almost immediately. Johnson died tragically in a car wreck in the summer of 1938. Van Vechten was Johnson's literary executor, and established the James Weldon Johnson Collection of Negro Arts and Letters in his honor at Yale University. Van Vechten called his friend "a well-nigh perfect human being."

10 *Katharine Cornell,* January 10, 1933
14" x 11"

Cornell (1893-1974) was one of the most celebrated performers on the American stage. She made her theater debut in New York in 1916, and won critical praise three years later in London for her part in *Little Women.* Among her finest performances were roles in *The Barretts of Wimpole Street* (1931) and *Romeo and Juliet* (1933). She toured extensively in these and many subsequent productions until her retirement in 1961. In printing this image Van Vechten cropped his negative considerably to isolate Cornell's head dramatically against a solid background of shadow.

11 *Ina Claire,* October 31, 1932
14" x 11"

One of the finest comedic performers on the American stage, Ina Claire (1892-1985) was praised for her urbane and witty style. She entered show business at the age of thirteen and performed on the vaudeville circuit, in musicals, and in the Ziegfeld Follies. She gained wide notice for her title role in the 1917 comedy *Polly With a Past.* Her many other stage credits included *The Awful Truth* (1922), *The Last of Mrs. Cheyney* (1925), *Our Betters* (1928), *Biography* (1932), *End of Summer* (1936), *Barchester Towers* (1937), and *The Talley Method* (1941). She made her last Broadway appearance in 1954. Claire also appeared in nine films, including *The Awful Truth* (1929), *Ninotchka* (1939), and *Claudia* (1943). This image, drawn from a lengthy session involving various poses and costume changes, presents Claire's face as a luminous element in a carefully constructed formal arrangement.

12 *Ona Munson,* November 1, 1932
9" x 63/4"

Munson (1906-1955) was an actress of moderate renown who worked in film, theater, radio, and television. She began in vaudeville in 1922. By 1925 she was playing the title role in a touring production of *No, No, Nanette,* which subsequently appeared in New York. She performed in numerous other plays, and acted in such films as *Gone With The Wind.* She was married to the artist and designer Eugene Berman.

13 *Claire Luce,* June 14, 1933

13⅝" x 10⅞"

Luce (1904-1989) studied dance as a child in Ludlow, Massachusetts, and ran away to New York City as a teenager to enter show business. She starred in productions by Florenz Ziegfeld in 1926-27, and was paired with Fred Astaire in *The Gay Divorcée,* which played both on Broadway and in London. Luce was appearing in *Of Mice and Men* in London at the outbreak of World War II. She spent the war in Britain, endured the London blitz, and entertained American and British troops. She became the first American actress to play leading roles at the Shakespeare Memorial Theater in Stratford-on-Avon, and continued to perform Shakespeare in the years following the war.

14 *George Gershwin,* March 28, 1933

14" x 11"

Gershwin (1898-1937) was one of the most important and popular American composers of his time. He incorporated the influences of jazz and popular music and wrote primarily for the Broadway musical theater. Born in Brooklyn, Gershwin took an interest in music at the age of twelve. He began playing piano and writing songs as a teenager, and by the time he was twenty had achieved considerable recognition. Several years of praise for his work culminated in 1924 with his first major Broadway success, *Lady Be Good,* and the composition *Rhapsody in Blue.* Other major works included the musical satire *Of Thee I Sing* (1931), the orchestral work *An American in Paris* (1932), and the opera *Porgy and Bess* (1935). Gershwin nearly always collaborated with his brother, lyricist Ira Gershwin. Van Vechten was a great admirer and close friend of George Gershwin, and deeply mourned the composer's early death. In honor of his friend, Van Vechten established the George Gershwin Memorial Collection of Music and Musical Literature at Fisk University.

15 *George M. Cohan,* October 23, 1933

14" x 10¾"

Cohan (1878-1942), nicknamed "Yankee Doodle Dandy," was a beloved American songwriter, actor, playwright, and producer of musical comedies. He performed in vaudeville as a child. His first full-length play opened in New York in 1901, and he subsequently wrote such popular songs as "You're a Grand Old Flag," "Give My Regards to Broadway," "I'm a Yankee Doodle Dandy," and "Over There." His career was the subject of both a film, *Yankee Doodle Dandy* (1942), and a Broadway musical, *George M!* (1968).

16 *Cab Calloway,* January 12, 1933

9¾" x 7½"

The noted singer, bandleader, and actor Cab Calloway was born in Rochester, New York, in 1907. After working in Chicago, his first recognition came in 1928 when he introduced the song "Ain't Misbehavin'" in the all-black production of *Connie's Hot Chocolates* on Broadway. He became known as the "King of Hi De Ho," a phrase he used one night when he forgot the lyrics to a song. His recordings of "St. James Infirmary Blues" and his own song "Minnie the Moocher" achieved great popularity. He appeared in several films in the 1930s and 1940s, and interrupted a successful nightclub career in 1952-54 to play in a world tour of Gershwin's *Porgy and Bess.* While unusual in Van Vechten's work, the extreme dynamism of this image represents a powerful and original interpretation of Calloway's exuberant energy.

17 *H. L. Mencken,* July 19, 1932

9¾" x 7⅜"

Henry Louis Mencken (1880-1956) was an outspoken journalist and commentator on American life. He began as a reporter for the Baltimore *Morning Herald,* and worked most of his career for the *Baltimore Sun.* With George Jean Nathan, he edited the influential journal *The Smart Set* (1914-1923), and from 1924 to 1933 he served as editor of the *American Mercury.* His book *The American Language,* published in 1919 and revised and supplemented over the years, brought Mencken recognition as a leading authority on the subject. His published works also include a three-volume autobiographical trilogy (1940-1943). In his many newspaper columns and reviews, Mencken lampooned nearly all aspects of American society, including organized religion, big business, and the values of the middle class. His outrageous style was popular in the 1920s, but slipped from favor in the hard times of depression and war. Van Vechten had known Mencken since the 1910s, and this portrait was made in Van Vechten's apartment after a dinner party for Mencken and his wife.

18 *Lincoln Kirstein,* May 8, 1933

9¾" x 6⅝"

Kirstein (b. 1907) is a talented writer and authority on the visual and performing arts. As an undergraduate at Harvard University he founded and edited the journal *Hound and Horn.* In 1933 he persuaded George Balanchine to come to the United States, and in the next few years the two collaborated to found the School of American Ballet and the various companies that became the New York City Ballet. Kirstein wrote the text for Walker Evans' seminal book, *American Photographs* (1938), edited the journal *Dance Index* (1942-1948), and, after World War II, also founded the Ballet Society. In recent years he published monographs on Nijinsky and Paul Cadmus. Van Vechten first met Kirstein in 1926 during the latter's freshman year at Harvard. They corresponded regularly in later years, primarily on matters related to dance. After Van Vechten's death in 1964 Kirstein wrote an eloquent memorial in his honor.

19 *Theodore Dreiser,* November 8, 1933
   14" X 11"

Theodore Dreiser (1871-1945) was perhaps the greatest American exponent of literary naturalism. From a poor family, Dreiser became a journalist in the Midwest before arriving in New York in 1894. He worked as a magazine editor while composing his first novel, *Sister Carrie,* which sold poorly on its publication in 1900. Later books include *The Financiers* (1912), *The Titan* (1914), and the highly praised and successful *An American Tragedy* (1925). Dreiser was one of the first people Van Vechten met on his arrival in New York City.

20 *Eugene O'Neill,* September 5, 1933
   14" X 11"

The son of a successful actor, Eugene O'Neill (1888-1953) became one of the finest dramatists in American history. As a young man O'Neill lived a derelict's life as a migratory and often alcoholic seaman. After a near-fatal bout with tuberculosis he began to write plays. He polished his technique with a year of study at Harvard University. The first performance of one of his works occurred in 1916 at an experimental theater in Provincetown, Massachusetts. His reputation grew steadily in the following years with such works as *Beyond the Horizon* (1920), *The Emperor Jones* (1920), *Anna Christie* (1922), *Desire Under the Elms* (1924), *Strange Interlude* (1928), *Mourning Becomes Electra* (1931), *Ah! Wilderness* (1933), *The Iceman Cometh* (1946), and *Long Day's Journey Into Night* (performed posthumously in 1956). In the course of his celebrated career O'Neill won four Pulitzer Prizes and the Nobel Prize for Literature. Despite this success, O'Neill's life was deeply troubled by unhappy marriages and great bitterness in his later years.

21 *Marcel Duchamp,* November 17, 1933
   9³/₈" X 7³/₈"

Duchamp (1887-1968) was one of the most original and influential artists of this century. His Cubist painting *Nude Descending a Staircase No. 2* (1912) had been the sensation of the 1913 Armory Show, and his most important artistic works were created within the following decade. The elegant simplicity of his "readymades" and the densely layered meanings of his monumental construction *The Large Glass* (1913-1923) changed the course of modern art history. While Duchamp continued to make art after 1923, he did so quietly, and spent most of his time on the cerebral pleasures of chess. In making this print Van Vechten cropped his negative considerably to center and monumentalize Duchamp's dramatically illuminated profile.

22 *Cesar Romero,* February 23, 1934
   9¹/₂" X 7¹/₂"

Romero (b. 1907) began as a dancer and Broadway actor before achieving fame in Hollywood. His lengthy motion picture career began with such films as *The Thin Man* (1934), *Metropolitan* (1935), and *The Return of the Cisco Kid* (1939). He went on to appear in many other films and television programs. This portrait was made before Romero left New York for Hollywood.

23 *James Stewart,* October 15, 1934
   13⁷/₈" X 10⁷/₈"

One of America's best loved actors, James Stewart (b. 1908) began acting while studying architecture at Princeton University. He graduated in 1932, in the depths of the Depression, and scraped by on acting and stage managing jobs. By 1934, when Van Vechten made this portrait, Stewart was performing on Broadway in such productions as *Yellow Jack, All Good Americans,* and *Journey by Night.* He was discovered by Hollywood in 1935 and began one of the most distinguished American film careers. He appeared in a number of motion pictures in the next few years, including *Mister Smith Goes to Washington* (1940), *Destry Rides Again* (1940), and *The Philadelphia Story* (1940), for which he received an Oscar as best actor. Stewart served in the Air Force during World War II, reaching the rank of colonel. With the resumption of his film career, Stewart went on to appear in some of the most popular and acclaimed motion pictures of the era. Some of these include *It's a Wonderful Life* (1947), *Broken Arrow* (1950), *Harvey* (1950), *The Greatest Show on Earth* (1952), *Rear Window* (1954), *The Man from Laramie* (1954), *The Spirit of St. Louis* (1957), *Vertigo* (1958), *Anatomy of a Murder* (1959), *How the West was Won* (1962), and *The Flight of the Phoenix* (1965).

24 *Fania Marinoff,* February 25, 1934
   13⁷/₈" X 11"

Fanny Marinoff (1887-1971) was born in Odessa, Russia, and came to Boston at an early age. While living with her older brothers in Denver she discovered her interest in performing. Her first stage role, at the age of eight, was a child's part in *Cyrano de Bergerac.* She loved the experience and resolved to make acting her life. Marinoff honed her craft through years of experience in stock company productions in Denver and on the road. She came to New York City in 1903, and found substantial, if not starring, roles in several notable productions. She then went on tour to the West Coast (during which time she changed her name to Fania) and Chicago. Her first significant New York success was *The House Next Door,* which played for two years. The first of her numerous film roles came in the spring of 1914. Marinoff continued to work frequently on stage and in films through the early 1920s, and then intermittently until 1945. Marinoff married Van Vechten on October 21, 1914. While their schedules and interests prompted them to lead relatively independent lives, the two remained devoted to each other through a half-century of wedded life.

25 *Charles Henri Ford,* November 14, 1934
14" x 11"

A man of varied talents, Ford (b. 1913) is generally recognized as the first American Surrealist poet. He was also an editor, artist, and filmmaker. He edited the avant-garde journals *Blues: A Magazine of New Rhythms* (1929-30), and *View* (1940-47), both of which promoted the most challenging modern art and literature of the time. His later work includes photographs, collages, paintings, and lithographs, as well as efforts in film and multimedia events. Numerous collections of his poetry have been published, including *A Pamphlet of Sonnets* (1936), and *The Garden of Disorder and Other Poems* (1938). Highly peripatetic, Ford has lived outside the United States for various periods in France, Morocco, Italy, and Nepal. Van Vechten first had contact with Ford in 1933 when Gertrude Stein encouraged the younger man to send Van Vechten a sample of his writing. This photograph was made soon after Ford returned to New York from a three-year residence in Paris.

26 *Gertrude Stein in her lecture robes,* November 4, 1934
14" x 11"

The avant-garde writer Gertrude Stein (1874-1946) was born in Allegheny, Pennsylvania, and grew up in Vienna, Paris, and Oakland, California. At Radcliffe College she studied psychology with the philosopher William James. After medical studies at Johns Hopkins she went to Paris, where she lived first with her brother, the art collector and critic Leo Stein, and then with her longtime companion Alice B. Toklas. Stein became familiar with the most advanced visual art and literature of the period and her artistic judgments were highly regarded. Her own writing applied concepts from the visual arts to produce texts characterized by fragmentation, repetition, and abstraction. While influential within avant-garde circles, the difficulty of such volumes as *Tender Buttons* (1914) or *The Making of Americans* (1925) worked against any real popularity. Her book *The Autobiography of Alice B. Toklas* (1933) was one of her few publications to reach a wide audience. Van Vechten met Stein in 1913 and the two became lifelong friends. He provided unfailing encouragement and was tireless in promoting her work to editors and publishers in New York. He also accompanied her on several legs of her successful 1934-35 lecture tour of America. This tour had been prompted by the reception of *The Autobiography of Alice B. Toklas* and the success of the opera *Four Saints in Three Acts* (1934), a collaboration between Stein and composer Virgil Thomson. This image, depicting Stein in her formal lecture robes, was made at the beginning of her American lecture tour.

27 *Willa Cather,* January 22, 1936
9⅞" x 8"

The novelist Willa Cather (1873-1947) was best known for her portrayals of settlers and frontier life on the American plains. She grew up in rural Nebraska in a community of immigrants from Sweden, Bohemia, Russia, and Germany. After studies at the University of Nebraska, she worked as a teacher and magazine editor before devoting herself completely to her own writing. Her first volume of verse was published in 1903 during her employment as a teacher. Her early novels include *Alexander's Bridge* (1912), *O Pioneers!* (1913), *My Antonia* (1918), and *One of Ours* (1922), which won a Pulitzer Prize. She received additional renown with *A Lost Lady* (1923), which mourned the passing pioneer spirit of the Midwest. Later works such as *Death Comes for the Archbishop* (1927) and *Shadows on the Rock* (1931) dealt with more historical themes. Cather was one of Van Vechten's more reluctant sitters, and agreed to pose only at the urging of Alfred A. Knopf.

28 *W. Somerset Maugham, Park Square Garden, London,* May 26, 1934
14" x 9¼"

William Somerset Maugham (1874-1965) was an admired author of plays, short stories, and novels. He studied to be a doctor, but abandoned medicine after the modest success of his first play, *Liza of Lambeth* (1897). In 1908 he achieved a theatrical triumph–and financial security–by having four of his plays in production at the same time in London. He traveled widely after World War I and settled in a villa in the south of France. His major books include *Of Human Bondage* (1915), *The Moon and Sixpence* (1919), *Cakes and Ale* (1930), and *The Razor's Edge* (1944). He worked in a clear and unadorned style with a shrewd understanding of human nature. Van Vechten first met Maugham in the early 1920s through their mutual friend Avery Hopwood, and always appreciated the fact that Maugham had written positively of *The Tattooed Countess.*

29 *Ethel Merman in* Anything Goes, March 27, 1935
9⅝" x 7¼"

The singer and actress Ethel Merman (1909-1984) played the leading role in more than a dozen Broadway musicals. Her 1930 stage debut in George Gershwin's *Girl Crazy* was celebrated for her rendition of "I Got Rhythm." Merman became a favored performer of such major songwriters of the period as Gershwin, Irving Berlin, and Cole Porter. Her major stage successes included *Anything Goes* (1934), *Red, Hot and Blue* (1936), *Du Barry Was a Lady* (1939), *Panama Hattie* (1940), *Something for the Boys* (1943), *Annie Get Your Gun* (1946), and *Gypsy* (1959). In 1972 she received a special Tony award for lifetime achievement in the theater. This "environmental" portrait is unusual in Van Vechten's work, but he used the dramatic ambient light of the theater and the slight blur of the figure to evocative visual effect.

30 *Georgia O'Keeffe on the roof of her penthouse,* New York,
June 5, 1936
7³/₄" x 9⁵/₈"

O'Keeffe (1887-1986) was one of the most important American painters of this century. After studies at the Art Institute of Chicago and the Art Students' League of New York, O'Keeffe taught at various schools in Texas and other southern states. In 1916 Alfred Stieglitz saw her work for the first time and exhibited her drawings in his New York gallery. The two were married in 1924, and Stieglitz's extended photographic portrait of O'Keeffe constitutes one of the great artistic statements in modern photography. O'Keeffe spent summers in New Mexico, moving there permanently after Stieglitz's death in 1946. Her best-known paintings charge the motifs of the desert–flowers, bones, clouds, or the landscape itself–with psychological and symbolic power. This photograph, taken while O'Keeffe still maintained a New York residence, depicts her with a symbol of her beloved New Mexico. Van Vechten was instrumental in persuading O'Keeffe to donate parts of the Stieglitz archive to Yale University Library and Fisk University. Van Vechten's portraits of O'Keeffe were published in the February 14, 1938, issue of *Life.*

31 *Salvador Dali and Man Ray, Paris,* June 16, 1934
9¹/₄" x 13⁷/₈"

Salvador Dali (1904-1989) was a pioneer of European Surrealism and one of the most widely recognized artists of the modern era. Dali showed a precocious artistic talent as a child in his native city of Figueras, Spain. He arrived in Paris in 1928, and his first exhibition there a year later was a resounding success. In addition to his paintings, Dali is remembered for his collaboration with Luis Buñuel on two important Surrealist films: *Un Chien Andalou* (1929) and *L'Age D'Or* (1931). Dali's paintings were first shown in New York in 1933 at the Julien Levy Gallery. He became a familiar figure to Americans in the following years, as much for his flamboyant persona and outrageous pronouncements as for his art. By the 1940s his critical reputation had begun to decline even as his celebrity continued to grow.

Man Ray (1890-1976) was one of the most important American modernist artists. Prolific and endlessly inventive, he was a leading participant in the Dadaist and Surrealist movements in Paris in the 1920s and 1930s. Born in Philadelphia, Man Ray studied art in New York and began his professional career as a graphic designer and typographer. He met Alfred Stieglitz in 1910 and was introduced to the work of leading European modernist painters. In 1915 he met Marcel Duchamp, who encouraged his experimental tendencies. He moved to Paris in 1921, making a living as a portrait and fashion photographer while devoting great energy to his own creative work. He soon was celebrated as a leading avant-garde artist and photographer, as well as a fine portraitist. He exhibited in the first Surrealist exhibit in Paris in 1925, and his work was shown in New York in 1932 at the Julien Levy Gallery. He fled the Nazi occupation of France in 1940 and lived in the United States for a decade before returning to Paris for the remainder of his life.

Van Vechten had known Man Ray for at least fifteen years when he made this photograph. When Van Vechten visited Man Ray's Paris studio he found him deep in conversation with the young Salvador Dali, then still little known outside the avant-garde art community. The two artists were happy to cooperate with Van Vechten's request for a dual portrait, and accompanied him out of the studio to a nearby street. Here Van Vechten posed them together, as evidence of their friendship, in front of a wall of posters he found appealing.

32 *Marsden Hartley,* June 7, 1939
13¹/₄" x 9³/₈"

Hartley (1877-1943) was a reclusive and talented painter who lived in New York and Maine. Alfred Stieglitz first showed his paintings in 1909, and remained a firm supporter for many years. Van Vechten met Hartley at about the time of Mabel Dodge's first "evenings" in the early 1910s. The two enjoyed each other's company and met occasionally in Alfred Stieglitz's gallery "291" or in the painting studio of mutual friend Florine Stettheimer. However, when they met accidentally on the grounds of the 1939 World's Fair it had been years since the two had seen each other. For this portrait, Van Vechten posed Hartley before the exterior white plaster wall of the fair's art building. He never photographed Hartley again.

33 *Jean Cocteau, Paris,* October 14, 1949
9¹/₄" x 6¹/₄"

Cocteau (1889-1963) was an important French poet, novelist, actor, painter, and film director. His first poems were published in 1905. Inspired by performances of the Ballets Russe, under the direction of Sergei Diaghilev, Cocteau created his first avant-garde ballet in 1917. During World War I he served as an ambulance driver, and this experience inspired his novel *Thomas l'imposteur* (1923). During the years of the war he came to know many of the leaders of the artistic avant-garde, including Pablo Picasso, Amedeo Modigliani, Max Jacob, and Guillaume Apollinaire. Included among his most important works are the poem *L'Ange Heurtebise* (1925), the play *Orpheus* (1926), and the novels *Les Enfants terribles* (1929) and *La Machine infernale* (1934).

34 *Feral Benga,* January 10, 1937
14" x 11"

Benga (dates unknown) was a dancer who served as a model for the African-American sculptor Richmond Barthé. In 1938 Barthé created a bronze of Fania Marinoff as "Ariel."

35 *Ethel Waters,* February 19, 1939
13⅞" x 9"

Waters (1896-1977) was a popular actress and singer. Born in Chester, Pennsylvania, Waters grew up in poverty. She made her first stage appearance on an amateur night in Philadelphia while working as a hotel maid. After further struggles she began playing in Harlem nightclubs. In about 1921 she made the initial recording issued on the Black Swan label, the first African-American record company. She first appeared on Broadway in 1927 in the all-black musical *Africana.* After hearing her sing "Stormy Weather" Irving Berlin signed Waters for *As Thousands Cheer* (1933), her first major Broadway success. One of her most notable stage performances came in the 1950 production of Carson McCullers's *The Member of the Wedding.* Waters also appeared in nine motion pictures, ranging from *On With the Show* (1929) to *The Sound and the Fury* (1959). She received Academy Award nominations for her roles in *Pinky* (1949), and the film version of *The Member of the Wedding* (1952). After being introduced to Waters' work by James Weldon Johnson, Van Vechten wrote an article on her for the March 1926 issue of *Vanity Fair.* By the following year the two had become good friends, and she often attended Van Vechten's parties.

36 *Bessie Smith,* February 3, 1936
9⅝" x 7⅝"

Smith (1894-1937) was one of the greatest and most influential American blues singers. Born into a poor family, Smith began singing in childhood and was encouraged by the older performer Ma Rainey. Smith spent several years traveling through the South to perform in saloons and small theaters. She was eventually discovered by a representative of Columbia Records and made her first recordings in February 1923. The "Empress of the Blues," as she became known, went on to record with many of the outstanding instrumentalists of the era, including Louis Armstrong, Fletcher Henderson, and Benny Goodman. Smith was a bold, confident, and earthy singer of enormous power. In addition to her extensive catalog of recordings, she appears in the short film *St. Louis Blues* (1929). Van Vechten was a great fan of Smith and owned copies of nearly all of her records. He played these for guests frequently, and Smith herself performed at one of Van Vechten's parties in April 1928.

37 *Thomas Mann,* April 20, 1937
14" x 11"

Thomas Mann (1875-1955) was one of the most important writers of this century. He worked in a subtle and finely crafted style that blended realism and symbolism. His most important early works include *Buddenbrooks* (1900), *Death in Venice* (1912), and *The Magic Mountain* (1924), and major essays on Tolstoy, Goethe, Freud, Nietzsche, and Wagner. Mann was awarded the Nobel Prize for literature in 1929. He lived in Munich until 1933, when his anti-Nazi sentiments forced him to leave his native country. Mann's remaining life was spent in Switzerland and the United States. His later works include four novels based on the biblical Joseph (1933-43), as well as *Doctor Faustus* (1948) and *The Confessions of Felix Krull, Confidence Man* (1954).

38 *Joe Louis,* September 15, 1941
13⅞" x 10⅞"

Joe Louis (1914-1981) was one of the greatest boxers of all time. His made his professional debut in 1934, and was generally considered to be at his athletic peak between 1939 and 1942. He held the heavyweight crown from 1937 until his retirement in 1949, the longest championship reign in the history of that division. In this period he defended his title twenty-five times in addition to serving in the Army during World War II. Louis's last major fight, a 1951 comeback attempt against Rocky Marciano, ended in defeat. This photograph was made at Louis's training camp at Greenwood Lake, New York. During this visit Van Vechten also photographed Louis in street clothes, and with his young visitor Lena Horne.

39 *Tennessee Williams,* November 14, 1948
10" x 8"

The dramatist Tennessee Williams (1911-1983) was famed for his tormented studies of human frustration and turmoil. He became interested in playwriting while studying at the University of Missouri (Columbia) and Washington University (St. Louis). Encouraged by his initial efforts, he earned a B.A. degree in dramatic writing at the University of Iowa in 1938. He worked at a variety of jobs, from theater usher to Hollywood scriptwriter, before achieving success with *The Glass Menagerie* in 1944. His next major work, *A Streetcar Named Desire* (1947), was awarded a Pulitzer Prize. The most successful of his later works were *Cat On a Hot Tin Roof* (1955) and *The Night of the Iguana* (1961). Williams struggled with ill-health and alcoholism in his later years.

40 *Evelyn Waugh,* November 15, 1948
14" x 10"

Waugh (1903-1966) was regarded as one of the most brilliant satirical novelists of his time. After studies at Oxford, and short stints as an art student and schoolmaster, he devoted himself to travel, observation, and writing. He soon earned praise for the sardonic wit and technical precision of his style. His early works–including *Decline and Fall* (1928), *Vile Bodies* (1930), *Black Mischief* (1932), *A Handful of Dust* (1934), and *Scoop* (1938)–are satirical distillations of first-hand observations. While *The Loved One* (1948) is in a similar vein, his post-war work was typified by a more serious tone. For example, *Brideshead Revisited* (1945) examined the faith of a Catholic family. In his trilogy *Men at Arms* (1952), *Officers and Gentlemen* (1955), and *Unconditional Surrender* (1961), Waugh examined World War II and some of its larger issues. His numerous other volumes include travel books and biographies.

41 *Thomas Wolfe,* April 14, 1937
14" x 10³⁄₈"

Wolfe (1900-1938) was born and raised in Asheville, North Carolina. While attending the University of North Carolina he wrote and acted in several short plays. After studying playwriting at Harvard, Wolfe moved to New York City to teach. In 1926 he began *Look Homeward Angel,* a fictional recasting of his own youth. The critical success of this book encouraged him to devote himself fully to writing. He subsequently published *Of Time and the River* (1935) and *The Story of a Novel* (1936). At his death in 1938, Wolfe left an enormous quantity of unfinished manuscripts. These were edited into two novels, *The Web and the Rock* (1939) and *You Can't Go Home Again* (1940), and several short stories.

42 *Charles Laughton,* April 4, 1940
10" x 8"

Charles Laughton (1899-1962) studied at the Royal Academy of Dramatic Art in London, and made a successful stage debut there in 1926. He came to New York in 1931 in *Payment Deferred,* and became a United States citizen nineteen years later. He is best known for his lengthy film career. He received international recognition and an Oscar for his performance in *The Private Life of Henry VIII* (1933), and also played lead roles in *Mutiny on the Bounty* (1935) and *Ruggles of Red Gap* (1935). In addition to playing characters as diverse as Rembrandt and Quasimodo, Laughton directed the critically acclaimed film *The Night of the Hunter* (1955). His later films included *Witness for the Prosecution* (1957), *Spartacus* (1960), and *Advise and Consent* (1962).

43 *Robert Earl Jones, in Langston Hughes's* Don't You Want to be Free?, June 23, 1938
14 x 11"

Jones (b. 1900), a native of Mississippi, first achieved recognition as an actor in New York in 1936. His early stage credits include *Of Mice and Men* and *Don't You Want to be Free?,* and the title roles in *Othello* and *The Emperor Jones.* He appeared in a number of other theater productions as well as such films as *Lying Lips* (1939), *The Notorious Elinor Lee* (1940), *Odds Against Tomorrow* (1959), *Wild River* (1960), *Mississippi Summer* (1971), and *The Sting* (1974). He also taught at Wesleyan University and the City University of New York. His son, James Earl Jones, was born in 1931.

44 *Lillian Gish,* October 28, 1947
10" x 8"

Gish (b. 1896) began in show business at the age of five with her sister Dorothy. Her theater debut came in 1913 and she went on to a lengthy career on the stage and in film and television. She first achieved fame in a series of spectacular silent films by D.W. Griffith: *The Birth of a Nation* (1915), *Intolerance* (1916), *Broken Blossoms* (1919), and *Orphans of the Storm* (1921). Other films followed, and she resumed her stage career in 1930. Her performance in the play *The Trip to Bountiful* (1953) was particularly praised.

45 *Truman Capote,* March 30, 1948
9³⁄₄" x 6³⁄₄"

The product of a broken home, Truman Capote (1924-1984) grew up with relatives in small towns in Louisiana and Alabama. He determined at an early age to become a writer and had his first story published as a teenager. He achieved wide critical praise at the age of twenty-three for his first novel, *Other Voices, Other Rooms* (1948). This was followed by *A Tree of Night* (1949), *The Glass Harp* (1951), and *Breakfast at Tiffany's* (1958). His immensely popular book *In Cold Blood* (1965) pioneered a genre he termed "the nonfiction novel." He also wrote the screenplay for the film *Beat the Devil* (1954) and collaborated with photographer Richard Avedon on the book *Observations* (1959). Capote battled various personal problems in his later years. At the time of his death, his large novel *Answered Prayers* remained unfinished. Capote's statement that he had "a love affair with cameras–all cameras," suggests Van Vechten's own enthusiasm for the images of celebrity.

46 *Marlon Brando in* A Streetcar Named Desire, December 27, 1948
12⁵⁄₈ x 9"

The son of a salesman and an actress, Marlon Brando (b. 1924) grew up in Illinois. After attending the Dramatic Workshop in New York City, he took various bit parts before receiving great critical praise for his portrayal of Stanley Kowalski in the Broadway premiere of Tennessee Williams's *A Streetcar Named Desire.* The earliest of his many films include *A Streetcar Named Desire* (1951), *Viva Zapata!* (1952), *Julius Caesar* (1953), *On The Waterfront* (1954), and *The Wild One* (1954).

47 *Tyrone Power and Judith Anderson in* John Brown's Body, March 3, 1950
13¹⁄₄" x 9¹⁄₄"

Tyrone Power (1914-1958) continued in the footsteps of his father and grandfather by becoming an actor. His career, which began slowly in 1931, was given a boost by Katharine Cornell's recommendation of him for parts in 1935 and 1936. His reputation on the Broadway stage led to success in Hollywood, where he came to fill the kinds of roles previously played by Rudolph Valentino and Douglas Fairbanks, Sr. One of his first films, *Lloyds of London* (1936), was an immediate success, and he went on to appear in more than forty motion pictures. His career was interrupted by four years of wartime service in the Marine Corps. He died unexpectedly, at the age of forty-four, after falling ill on a film set in Spain.

48 *Ossie Davis as Gabriel in* The Green Pastures, *April 12, 1951*
13⅝" x 9⅜"

The noted actor, director, and writer Ossie Davis was born in Georgia in 1917. After attending Howard and Columbia universities, Davis studied acting with the Rose McClendon Players in Harlem. He served in the army during World War II, and made his Broadway debut in 1946 in *Jeb Turner*. This play was short-lived, but he met Ruby Dee, a fellow member of the cast, and the two were married two years later. Davis struggled in the 1950s. He appeared in a 1951 cast of *Green Pastures* and won the title role in Kraft Theater's television production of *The Emperor Jones* (1955), but important roles for black actors remained few and far between. He fared better in the 1960s with appearances in such television programs as "The Defenders," "The Doctors," "The Fugitive," "Run for Your Life," and "Bonanza," and in several Hollywood films. His desire to be a writer finally came to fruition with his successful play *Purlie Victorious* which subsequently became the film *Gone Are the Days* and the smash Broadway musical *Purlie*. In the 1970s he also directed several films, including *Cotton Comes to Harlem* (1970).

49 *Pearl Bailey,* July 5, 1946
9¾" x 6⅜"

Born in Newport News, Virginia, Bailey (1918-1990) began performing as a child. Her great sense of timing, comic technique, and appealing singing voice all combined to make her a vibrant presence on nightclub stages, record, and film. Van Vechten photographed Bailey at the time of her 1946 Broadway debut in *St. Louis Woman*. Other stage credits include *Arms and the Man* (1950), *Bless You* (1950), *House of Flowers* (1954), and the title role in the all-black version of *Hello Dolly* (1967). Her film work included *Variety Girl* (1947), *Isn't It Romantic* (1948), *Carmen Jones* (1954), *Porgy and Bess* (1959), *That Certain Feeling* (1956), *St. Louis Blues* (1958), *All the Fine Young Cannibals* (1960), and *The Landlord* (1970). She became one of America's best-known black television stars through early appearances on the Ed Sullivan and Milton Berle variety shows, as well as many other programs. This unusual figure study was made in a session in which Bailey also posed in her costume for *St. Louis Woman*.

50 *Marian Anderson,* July 17, 1947
9⅜" x 7⅜"

One of the finest contraltos of her time, Marian Anderson (b. 1902) achieved recognition during several trips to Europe in the late 1920s and early 1930s. In 1939 she was prohibited because of her race from singing at Constitution Hall in Washington, D.C. Outraged at this decision by the D.A.R., a citizens group, including Eleanor Roosevelt, organized a concert for Anderson at the Lincoln Memorial. This drew an enormous crowd of 75,000 and was a spectacular success. Van Vechten heard her perform many times and had enormous respect for her talent, commitment, and quiet dignity.

51 *Billie Holiday,* March 23, 1949
13⅞" x 9"

Billie Holiday (1915-1959) was one of the greatest jazz singers in history. Although never formally trained, she became known for the power and emotion of her voice, and the technical complexity of her phrasing. As a child, growing up under very difficult circumstances, she heard recordings by Bessie Smith and Louis Armstrong. Her professional singing debut came in 1931 in obscure Harlem nightclubs. She worked without much recognition until 1935, but had become a solo attraction by 1940. Her later career was dominated by a struggle with heroin addiction. Van Vechten heard Holiday sing many times. He only portrayed her once, however, in an emotionally draining session of photography and conversation that lasted from 8 o'clock one evening to 5 a.m. the next morning. (This session was described at length in Van Vechten's "Portraits of the Artists," *Esquire,* December 1962.)

52 *James Baldwin,* September 13, 1955
10" x 7"

Baldwin (1924-1987) was an important essayist, novelist, playwright, and spokesman on issues of racial justice. He grew up poor in Harlem, the eldest of nine children. As a teenager he served as a preacher in a small revivalist church and this experience was reflected in his book *Go Tell It on the Mountain* (1953) and the play *The Amen Corner* (first performed in 1965). His collection of essays, *Notes of a Native Son* was published in 1955, followed a year later by his novel *Giovanni's Room*. He lived in Paris from 1948 to 1957. Upon returning to New York in 1957 Baldwin became active in the growing civil rights movement. His book of essays, *Nobody Knows My Name* (1961) explored the complex nature of race relations in America. This theme was further explored in *Another Country* (1962) and *The Fire Next Time* (1963). His later works included *Going to Meet the Man* (1965) and *Tell Me How Long the Train's Been Gone* (1968). Baldwin admired Van Vechten's portraits and used one from this sitting on the dust jacket of his 1956 book.

53 *Dizzy Gillespie,* December 2, 1955
12¾" x 9⅛"

The trumpeter, composer, and bandleader Dizzy Gillespie (b. 1917) was an important pioneer of modern jazz. He worked with several bands in the late 1930s, including that of Cab Calloway, before becoming part of the nascent be-bop scene in New York with pianist Thelonius Monk, drummer Kenny Clarke, and saxophonist Charlie Parker. Gillespie's brilliant technique and range of musical ideas influenced several subsequent generations of younger trumpeters.

54 *Harry Belafonte in* John Murray Anderson's Almanac,
February 18, 1954
14" x 9¼"

Harry Belafonte (b. 1927) was one of the first blacks to become a leading man in Hollywood films. He made his film debut in *Bright Road* (1953), and played important roles in *Carmen Jones* (1954), *Island in the Sun* (1957), *The World, the Flesh, and the Devil* (1959), and *Odds Against Tomorrow* (1959). In the 1960s he devoted considerable energy to the cause of civil rights and worked closely with Dr. Martin Luther King, Jr. In the 1970s he returned to films as both actor and producer in *Angel Levine* (1970) and *Buck and the Preacher* (1972). He appeared on many television programs and was also known for his smoky-voiced rendition of romantic ballads. Van Vechten's notes indicate that this image depicts Belafonte in "West Indian costume." The patterned backdrop and unconventional pose combine to create an intriguingly offbeat effect.

55 *Leontyne Price in* Porgy and Bess, May 19, 1953
12⅞" x 8¾"

The talent of Leontyne Price (b. 1927) was recognized when she was a child. She made her professional debut in New York in 1952 after studying at the Juilliard School of Music. Ira Gershwin selected her to sing Bess in a revival of *Porgy and Bess.* This success led to tours of the United States and Europe. She became the first African-American to sing opera on television in NBC's 1955 production of *Tosca.* She made her debut at the Metropolitan Opera in 1961 and went on to become one of the Met's leading sopranos. Price worked all her life against racial prejudice and always invested her parts with sophistication and dignity. This photograph, depicting Price in a more mischievous mood, was made at the beginning of her professional career.

56 *Diahann Carroll,* March 14, 1955
10" x 7⅜"

Diahann Carroll was born in New York City in 1935 as Carol Diann Johnson, the daughter of a subway conductor. She began her career as a model and developed an image of flawless glamour. Carroll first achieved recognition for her work on the stage in the 1954 show *House of Flowers.* Her subsequent film work includes *Carmen Jones* (1954), *Porgy and Bess* (1959), *Paris Blues* (1961), *Hurry Sundown* (1967), *The Split* (1968), and *Claudine* (1974), for which she received an Oscar nomination. She also made television appearances on variety shows and in series such as "Dynasty." Her own series, "Julia," ran from 1968 to 1971.

57 *James Earl Jones,* May 29, 1961
9½" x 7½"

One of the best-known contemporary actors, Jones (b. 1931) has appeared in numerous stage, film, and television productions. The son of actor Robert Earl Jones, he graduated from the University of Michigan before studying act-

ing with Lee Strasberg. His first significant part was in the New York Shakespeare Festival's *Romeo and Juliet* in 1955. He subsequently appeared in a number of other Shakespearean productions, including the title roles in *Othello, Macbeth,* and *King Lear.* Jones received critical praise in 1968 for his role as boxing champion Jack Johnson in the play *The Great White Hope.* His film credits include *Dr. Strangelove* (1964), *Comedians* (1967), *The Great White Hope* (1970), *The Man* (1972), *The River Niger* (1976), and *The Bingo Long Traveling All-Stars and Motor Kings* (1976). He has also become a familiar presence on television. He was one of the first black actors cast in a regular role on a soap opera ("The Guiding Light" in 1967), and appeared in the popular miniseries "Roots" (1979).

58 *Gloria Vanderbilt,* May 23, 1958
10" x 8"

Gloria Vanderbilt di Cocco Stokowski Lumet Cooper (b. 1924) first achieved celebrity as "The Poor Little Rich Girl" at the center of a sensational custody trial. She was the daughter of Gloria Morgan Vanderbilt, an international beauty and celebrity. In 1934 the latter's sister-in-law, Gertrude Vanderbilt Whitney, known as the richest woman in America, sued for custody of young Gloria, citing the poor influence of her mother's lifestyle. The resulting trial captured the attention of the nation. Gloria Vanderbilt continued to make news as an adult for her multiple marriages and later business career in cosmetics, perfume, and fashion jeans. Van Vechten photographed Vanderbilt during the time of her marriage to director Sidney Lumet, when she was doing some acting on stage and in television.

59 *Mahalia Jackson,* April 16, 1962
13½" x 9⅛"

Jackson (1911-1972) was an intensely devout and talented religious vocalist. Born in New Orleans as the granddaughter of a slave, she began singing in the church choir as a child. In the early 1930s she took part in a cross-country gospel crusade, singing in store-front churches and revival tents. Her powerful voice and passionate faith gave her an absolutely commanding presence and she quickly attracted attention in the black community with such songs as "He's Got the Whole World in His Hands." Her first recordings were made in 1934. While the religious nature of her music limited Jackson's appeal outside the African-American community, her reputation grew steadily. In 1950 she made a smashing debut at Carnegie Hall. She began overseas tours in 1952, appearing in Japan, India, and Europe. Jackson devoted great energy in the last decade of her life to the cause of civil rights. She was closely associated with the Rev. Dr. Martin Luther King, Jr., and sang at his celebrated March on Washington in 1963. She gave numerous benefit performances and was widely revered for her talent, personal dignity, and selfless commitment to social justice.